GERMAN EXPRESSIONISM

Jack O'Connell
Portland
27. Dezember 1996

GERMAN EXPRESSIONISM

Series edited by J. M. Ritchie

VISION AND AFTERMATH

Four Expressionist War Plays

Translated from the German by J. M. Ritchie and J. D. Stowell

Introduced by J. M. Ritchie

CALDER AND BOYARS · LONDON

First published in Great Britain 1969 *by*
Calder and Boyars Ltd.,
18 *Brewer Street, London W*1

© *These translations, Calder and Boyars* 1969

Krieg, Ein Tedeum by Carl Hauptmann, first published 1914 by Kurt Wolff Verlag, and now available in *Schrei und Behenntnis,* ed. Karl Otten, Hermann Luchterhand Verlag, 1959, is published here by arrangement with the copyright owner, Prof. Dr Peuckert, 61 Darmstadt-Mühlthal, Engelsmühle, Germany.

Seeschlacht by Reinhard Goering, from *Deutsches Theater des Expressionismus,* ed. Joachim Schondorff, Munich 1962, is published by arrangement with Albert Langen – George Muller Verlag. Performing rights are controlled by S. Fischer Verlag, Frankfurt.

Antigone by Walter Hasenclever, from *Walter Hasenclever: Gedichte, Dramen, Prosa,* Rowohlt Verlag, 1963, is published by arrangement with the copyright owner, Edith Hasenclever, Cagnes-sur-Mer.

Hinkemann by Ernst Toller, from *Ernst Toller: Prosa, Briefe, Dramen, Gedichte,* Rowohlt Verlag, 1961, is published by arrangement with the copyright owner, Sidney Kaufman, 14 Fairway Close, Forest Hills 75, N.Y., U.S.A.

PRINTED IN GREAT BRITAIN BY
WILLMER BROTHERS LIMITED, BIRKENHEAD

CONTENTS

INTRODUCTION

Germany before the outbreak of the First World War was filled with a longing for change. People wanted something to happen —almost anything, to bring release from the oppressive traditions and conventions of the society they lived in. Life in Wilhelminian Germany meant for many a state of emptiness and boredom in which the dictum *Ruhe ist die erste Bürgerpflicht* still applied. Little wonder then that talk of *Aufbruch*, i.e. the need for a new start, a break with the old, was wide-spread and was not merely one of the many slogans coined by avant-garde contributors to Expressionist journals with inflammatory titles like *Storm* and *Action*. Indeed in a sense it is misleading to repeat the idea that the Expressionists were singled out from their contemporaries by their pre-visions of war, doom and destruction, chaos and annihilation, the twilight of man-kind,—they were merely giving their particular form of expression to much more widely held longings for release from unbearable restrictions. The war itself when it came surprised most, even those who had conjured up its spirit most vividly, but it was generally welcomed. The process of disillusionment, however, was extremely rapid when the dreamers and visionaries were confronted with the realities of modern warfare and not surprisingly this process is reflected in the literature and drama of the time which moved through the full range from patriotic enthusiasm to radical pacificism within the space of a few years. The tone changes quickly from excited pathos and emotional rhetoric to cold and disillusioned reporting.

Very few German war-books attained any literary value, though Erich Maria Remarque's *All Quiet on the Western Front*, written some years after the war (1929), did enjoy world success both as a novel and as a film surpassing even that of the French plea for general peace on which it is broadly based, namely Henri Barbusse's *Le Feu* (1916). Without any doubt, however, it was Ernst Jünger's *In Stahlgewittern* (1919), a report in diary form, which gave the best account of what it meant to be young before the war, to know this longing for *Aufbruch* and then to pass from first fine enthusiasm to the life of a front-line soldier in the living hell of continuous trench war-fare. The greatest dramatic work to emerge from the war was clearly Karl Kraus' *Last Days of Mankind* which dealt with the course of the war by quoting the actual words used by the newspapers, official communiqués, statesmen, soldiers and black marketeers of the time. This monumental work is therefore completely realistic, but at the same time it becomes Expressionistic by its sheer cosmic scope, especially in the apocalyptic vision of the epilogue entitled *The Last Night* which ends with the total destruction of the world through an invasion from Mars. Unfortunately the size of this Martian drama (1,000 pages approx.) makes its inclusion in this volume impossible and Kraus himself realised that no theatre on earth could ever play it in full.

Needless to say there was still much traditional drama in Germany, "of the historical type, evoking heroic figures from the national past". These plays about such figures as Frederick the Great and Bismarck continued to appear throughout the war and after it. But the number of anti-war plays of a quite revolutionary nature which were not only written, but published and produced in these years is one of the most remarkable features not only of the Expressionist movement but also of the German literary scene in general. H. F. Garten has discussed this curious state of affairs in his *Modern German Drama* and he points in particular to the play *War, A Te Deum* by Carl Hauptmann (1858-1921) as the starting-point for much that was to revolutionise the German drama. Carl Hauptmann, the older brother of the more famous Gerhart Hauptmann, is not normally associated with the Expressionist movement by critics and historians and even this war play still shows many traces of the Neo-Romantic generation to which he really belongs and whose style he exploited without great or lasting success in his other works. However, despite the florid language and the historical setting this play does represent a marked step forward towards the new Expressionist type of drama. Princess Kail is revealed in the very first words of the play as a visionary who already foresees "hosts of red and white assassins storming against each other," and the realism of the formal structure is early broken down by the arrival of beasts as the Great Powers to haggle over the partition of Europe, followed by a grotesque

European Reckoner and an Archangel. There is also clearly a sharp division between the older and younger generations as is shown by the conflict between Enoch Kail and his father; the young count is a youth frustrated beyond endurance by the society in which he is placed and filled with an irresistible impulse to know and enjoy life to the full. This indeed is why the young Jewess Gruschka loves him, because he revolts against the insipid and self-satisfied in life, because he demands the absolute. She, needless to say, is also a visionary like the boy's mother. Hence the play reveals the typically Expressionist themes, of lust for life even at the expense of total chaos, the impending twilight of mankind, and the visionary potential of man—combined with the anti-naturalistic treatment of them on the stage. All these were to become constants of the new revolutionary theatre. The suspicion in which reason, intellect and "common sense" are held in the Expressionist drama are also early demonstrated by the manner in which the forebodings of doom conjured up by the pressure of the Great Power Beasts in this castle are *not* removed by the arrival of the European Reckoner, who indeed only seems to show that reasons of mutual advantage and the like are not sufficient to stop the machine of war once it has begun to roll. This is presented in another section by the petit-bourgeois *rentier* illusion that "modern culture and civilisation must be beyond war" and that "if one weighs up and calculates the arguments for and against . . . war would be the most senseless waste of money . . . not just barbarism . . . the most criminal waste of money". Such 'we-are-all-reasonable-and-civilised-human-beings' arguments are demolished by the Archangel who simply strikes the European Reckoner down with his sword.

Princess Kail has visions, Gruschka has visions, and even Enoch has a glimpse of coming events—in Part Two the Archangel opens the eyes of yet another visionary Petrus Heissler. This time the biblical note is particularly indicative of later Expressionist drama not only in the language but also in the revelation of the beast in man which is let loose first on the domestic level with the drunkard who strangles his own wife, then on the national level as the youth of the country march off to war singing, while Petrus Heissler walks through the world as the prophet of doom announcing the coming of the Great War. War is therefore not

9

merely something inevitable, it is the will of God. Indeed just as the young Enoch longs for release from restrictive society in the explosion of war, so too God is proclaimed in the apocalyptic words of the Archangel as the great liberator and anarchist, the creator of chaos, the ultimate mystery far crueller than the forces of animality, the destroyer of a puny mankind that craves prosperity and comfort. He is the great incendiary who wants to measure out the limits of eternity. And yet His mysterious and ineluctable force is not purely destructive or chaotic, for God will cast Himself upon mankind like seed and out of the annihilation of millions a New Man will be born. With this the central motif of all Expressionist literature is struck—the birth of the New Man, the regeneration of mankind, in this case out of war. So war comes. Three Archangels with scrolls in their hands stride out of the village and disappear into the houses. Mankind cannot be tamed, the world moves apparently of its own volition into war. The Three Archangels meanwhile are followed by Three Horrific Figures who bring plague and pestilence to help the Big Blood Bath along—with typically Expressionistic exploitation of the 'grotesque'.

Part Three of Hauptmann's play is strangely prescient of Brecht's *Mother Courage* with its Canteen Woman following the campaigns of the wars. But the scene is really dominated by yet another seer, this time a Napoleon-like *Führer* who enslaves his people through the rhetoric with which he gives expression to his personal vision. War has now become personified in the figure of the great criminal, the great assassin who had been forged to the lonely rock in the ocean. This genius with the power to whirl up nations and kings into wild confusion in his lust for world domination is a fierce Baal-like monster who devours cities and lashes mankind on to drag his golden coach through streams of human blood and millions of crushed bodies. Resistance seems unthinkable and the end is inevitable—total destruction, the collapse of civilisation, the End of the World. Yet the exciting intoxication of blind violence and the abandonment of reason is contagious as long as it lasts. This conflict between the attractions of red-hot ecstasy (*Rausch*) on the one hand and cool reason on the other is one to which the Expressionists constantly returned. Very characteristic too is the extent to which music and song are used to reinforce the concrete imagery and visionary nature of the play. Hence

Part Three moves from the Mother Courage-like ballad of the Canteen Woman through the exultant war songs of the excited populace and thunderous choruses of Archangels down to funeral music swelling more and more horribly to presage the end. Instead of a radiant dawn into which the Napoleonic superman had promised to lead the people deepest darkness settles over the scene.

The Fourth and last part of the play is perhaps the least successful for it must demonstrate the Expressionistic belief in the regeneration of mankind through the purifying process of war. Hence the final 'twilight of mankind' is ambivalent signifying as here a vision of the end of the world, but also the possibility of a new dawn. As portrayed in Hauptmann's play the world looks as it might after a nuclear disaster—only a few cripples have survived and all distinctions of class, profession and nationality have been wiped out. Yet even now these seeds of conflict are latent in the survivors and the troubles that split the world apart can easily start up again and lead once more to war. So the dawn of a completely new age can only be ushered in by a new generation personified in the son born to Gruschka. The play finishes as it started on a biblical note with the birth of the New Man who is to be the saviour of mankind.

Clearly there are many weaknesses in this play, not least the ending, nevertheless Carl Hauptmann had in 1913 succeeded remarkably in giving expression not only to the tensions and forebodings of the years preceding the Great War but also to the subconscious longing for the chaos and violence that war would bring. There is an almost Germanic death-wish in the atmosphere which anticipates remarkably the abandonment of reason and the glad acceptance of a Hitler-inspired *Rausch* before the start of the Second World War. Although decidedly a representative of the older generation of dramatists in his choice of historical background for his war play, nevertheless in form and content Hauptmann broke much new ground for the coming revolutionary drama of the Twenties.

H. F. Garten has singled out the year 1916 as marking the turning point in the general attitude to the war. Until then support for the war had been wide-spread. But gradually "a premonition of coming disaster dawned upon the more far-sighted". From

1916 on, a stream of plays critical of the war was written, published and in some cases even produced despite the strict censorship. Of these the best known are Reinhard Goering's *Seeschlacht* (Naval Encounter), Stefan Zweig's *Jeremiah*, and Fritz von Unruh's *Ein Geschlecht* (One Family). Plays by Kaiser, *The Burghers of Calais* and the *Gas* trilogy, or by Sternheim e.g. *1913*, which also belong in this context will be discussed elsewhere in this series in separate volumes devoted to these dramatists.

Very much in the biblical strain of Hauptmann's *War, A Te Deum* is Zweig's *Jeremiah* which was the first clear denunciation of war in dramatic form. The rather over-elaborate, flowery rhetoric and emotional verse of this vast work have lost much of their power for the modern audience, nevertheless Garten has rightly singled out the powerful anti-war protest of some passages. As in *War* the people are easily swept along by the glorious visions conjured up by the war party. This time the true leader, however, is a prophetic seer who resists the trend of popular excitement and denounces war:

> War is a wild and wicked beast, he eats the flesh from the strong and sucks the marrow from the mighty ones, he crushes the cities between his jaws and with his hoofs he tramples the land.

The pacifist tendency is quite outspoken and the play ends with a rhapsodic plea for "a gospel of brotherhood and redemption through suffering. Defeat . . . is a blessing bestowed by God to purify the hearts of men". (Garten) So the purification motif is still powerful even in defeat. War is a devouring monster, a beast but it can also be portrayed as a machine, a mighty Juggernaut which once on the move rolls on irrevocably over puny mankind—this is the feeling imparted by Reinhard Goering's play *Naval Encounter* (1916-17). This drama is much more decidedly Expressionistic in form and content. The war is no longer fought round romantic Napoleonic bivouacs by colourful soldateska; it has become the mechanical warfare of the modern age. Not that this is presented with any realistic detail—on the contrary the stylisation is now complete, the compression to abstract form extreme, the process of depersonalisation total. The bare gun-turret and the menacing efficiency of the naval gun dominate the scene while the sailors serving it are reduced to numbers. In some productions of the play the gun is not even there—the puppet-like slaves go through the balletic motions of aiming and firing a non-existent gun while the action towards the end is punctuated by flashes, bangs and screams.

Goering's play is a typically Expressionistic scream-play (*Schreidrama*). The play begins with a shout and there are plenty of screams and shouts before the end. But despite this the striking feature of the play is the tight discipline and the controlled, hard, highly stylised language employed to express the feverish atmosphere of the situation. This is a marked development from the Neo-Romantic diction of Carl Hauptmann and the excessively flowery periods of Zweig's *Jeremiah*. Yet the prose is still poetic in the new Expressionist manner and can easily be printed in lines like verse. The quick switches from short, sharp stychomythic utterance of classical brevity to long monologues of considerable eloquence is a feature of the Expressionist style which revels in the conjunction of extremes—ice-cold with fever-heat, compression with expansiveness, logicality with ecstasy, static with dynamic. Characteristically too there is little or no plot—merely the suffocating situation of seven men moving towards apparently inevitable death. The talk is of signs at sea, girls, the enemy and death. Sleep alternates with wakefulness, dream with reality. The climax of the play is the discussion between the First Sailor and the Fifth Sailor round the problem of obedience or mutiny. Significantly the First Gunner is the religious seeker who keeps looking for a sign, and longs to know what the Higher Powers want of us, while the Fifth is the man who can no longer follow the instinctive behaviour patterns of his parents, the rationalist whose brain is surrounded by a buzzing swarm which threatens to suck it dry. He denies all knowledge of the Higher Powers. Totally Expressionistic is the Socratic dialogue which develops between these two men, where by a question-and-answer game an attempt is made to arrive at Truth. Must one obey if one's country commands? In the modern German context the question becomes particularly significant when the Fifth Gunner asks: "Can madness not reign over a whole nation and sway even its leader? Must we do the will of madmen?" What is the purpose of life on earth? To serve God as the First Gunner claims? To this problem the Fifth gives the typical Expressionist answer: "Not by having Him do you have all, but by being fully human." Here the untranslatable German *Mensch* is the key-word, namely self, individual, human-being, mortal, Man. The Socratic dialogue has now reached a point where war can be clearly denounced as madness and as a crime against mankind: "there is a certain bond between man and man; obeying it is a more sacred duty than anything else worth fighting for." With this conviction of the individual's duty towards his fellow men the Fifth Gunner can now express his determination to refuse to fight, he will mutiny even against "the merciless force, against something all are subject to, and everyone bows down to, . . . something no-one can revolt against." It is therefore always possible for the individual to assert himself and refuse to fight no matter how overwhelming the forces against him may be. At this point, however, the others awaken and overhear the mutinous talk and immediately it is demonstrated that talk and intellectual discussion are not the deciding factors, for even the firmest resolve cannot stand firm against the *Rausch* of action when enemy ships are sighted. Where till this point the play has been static, relying on the verbal exchanges of the seven, all now becomes dynamic as they prepare for battle. All are swept along by the feverish intoxication of battle *including* the Fifth Gunner. It is the test of battle which the Fourth says will show the New Man this age has produced. Action may mean death but for a brief moment one is living at fullest capacity. The Fifth Gunner now says: "I like action. It will cost us our lives any minute. But till then our lungs heave, hearts race, muscles jump. All that damned questioning, lads, where's it gone?" This is exactly the abandonment of reason portrayed in Hauptmann's play, exactly the same escape from the curse of excessive cerebration into hyperaemia, the blood-rush, the *Rausch* which led Gottfried Benn to accept at least for a time the Nazi mythology. By the end of the play the gunners are gas-masked and indistinguishably congealed into an anonymous fighting body. All individuality has been sacrificed to the group united in common action and all are soon dead or dying with the exception of the Fifth Gunner who is left to answer the question why he did not mutiny after all? He could have mutinied and it might have had some effect, but it is so much easier just to fire a gun, to submerge the individuality in the group allegiance, so much more difficult to stand out against one's fellows and the whole trend of the time. So the idea of mutiny raised in the play is lost again. Men are still no more than tiny cogs in a mighty war-machine over which they have no control. Can they even be held responsible for their actions?

See, see we did not choose the way, we had no power over the hands we raised. Yes, yes, we did do it, did act, did raise our hands. Ours is the guilt.

The whole work has the style and rigour of a classical tragedy with its constant suggestion of forces outside man (Higher Powers) controlling his destiny. Yet the final outcome is not fatalism but the idea that the individual must stand out against the forces that threaten to control him; he must act for the good of humanity in general. Man's duty to man is the final arbiter.

The classical style is also that adopted by Walter Hasenclever (1890-1940) for his anti-war *Antigone* which is, however, far more violent and outspoken than Goering's carefully balanced work. Hasenclever was already famous for his play *The Son* (1914) which with its characteristic father-son conflict gave early expression to the longing for escape into "life" felt by the younger generation and its reaction against the life-denying, rigid and stultifying bourgeois society exemplified by the father. *The Son* is clearly a work of protest with all the merits and demerits of Angry Young Man violence; even if its long and turbulent emotional monologues were all severely pruned the melodramatic excesses of the play could have little appeal to the present-day audience. With *Antigone*, however, Hasenclever moved from the middle-class milieu of his drama of social protest back to classical antiquity for his denunciation of war. His *Antigone* according to Garten "presents a perfect example of the Expressionist style: the language, austere and sparing, is shorn of all poetic adornments and occasionally rises to impassioned outbursts, always with the sole intention of conveying the author's message". In effect the play, like Goering's *Naval Encounter*, is characterised by the combination of extremes—classical brevity with long monologues, static and dynamic, logicality and ecstasy, etc. Now, however, instead of the stifling atmosphere of a naval gun-turret in a modern battle-ship Hasenclever, who was writing the play while with the German Army on the Eastern Front, constructed a play of vast scope and dimensions. Remembering a spectacular Reinhardt production of Sophocles' *Oedipus Rex* in a great hall, he wrote his *Antigone* for an amphitheatre. The stage is divided into two levels, a raised platform is the theatre of the king while an arena is the theatre of the people. Spotlights pick out this area or the other as required. The message of the play is the gospel of love and human brotherhood combined with a denunciation of war. Creon, the cruel king and tyrant, is given words of Emperor Wilhelm II to speak so that the contemporary reference is inescapable despite the classical setting. A striking feature of this play, as indeed of all Expressionist plays from Hauptmann's *War*, *A Te Deum* on, is that the People are presented as a more or less mindless mass to be moved in one direction or the other by the arguments of the opposing factions. In fact, despite the vast scope of the play and the *Sturm und Drang* violence with which the Antigone theme is treated, the play resolves itself into the typical Expressionist confrontation between two dominant personalities representative of dialectically opposed points of view, in this case Creon and Antigone. The people are swayed by them in one direction or the other. The play in essence progresses in a sequence of speech and counter-speech, argument and counter-argument until by the force of the dialectic even the tyrant Creon himself, who has lived by the dead letter of the law, is made to see the error of his ways and hand over power to the people. Antigone's eyes have been opened by the blind Oedipus who has shown her the nature of true human goodness and love and this in turn is the gospel she preaches to the masses. She conjures up apocalyptic images of the doom and destruction that ensue when mankind goes mad in war and warns the people against the easy temptation to revel in military glory. While the horrors of war conjured up by Antigone's words are powerful enough, in the following act another visionary arrives in the prophet Tiresias who is capable of creating a living image of war before the tyrant's eyes:

> *Heaps of dead. People with gaping wounds. Women, men with daggers in their chests. Demented, bleating like animals. Smashed limbs. Children stumble among the bodies.*

Typical too of the Expressionist drama is the exemplary suicide of Antigone—a strange way it might be thought to lead the way towards a regeneration of mankind, but the one taken by Eustache de Saint Pierre in Kaiser's *The Burghers of Calais*, Greta in Toller's *Hinkemann* and many other Expressionist visionaries. Antigone goes on ahead and is followed by Haemon, the king's son, who abandons the cult of the sword and kills himself beside her body after vainly stabbing at his tyrant father Creon. So "the first man of the new earth is converted by her grave." Also very characteristic of the Expressionist drama is the destruction of the city by fire with which the fourth act finishes. The Expressionist generation as has been seen was obsessed by the need for the eradication of the old way of life and constantly conjured up such images of the twilight of mankind. A new dawn is about to break, the rich and the mighty have fallen and the day of the people is at hand:

Palaces totter. Might has had its day.
He who was great, plunges to his doom,
The gates thunder shut.
He who possessed all, has lost all . . .
Follow me! I will lead you.
The wind rises from the ruins.
The new world dawns.

Creon voluntarily relinquishes power, his spirit broken by the deaths of Antigone, Haemon and his queen Eurydice. The new leader to emerge is a simple man of the people. Anarchy threatens but a voice from the tomb reminds mankind of the example of Antigone and all fall on their knees.

Clearly such a play is politically naïve, and melodramatically exaggerated in its piling up of horrors, warriors on horseback charging across the arena, visions of war, multiple deaths and extraordinary conversions. Nevertheless the exuberant theatricality of the play is equally not in doubt and strikingly reinforces the outspoken indictment of war.

From Hauptmann's war play on there had been in all Expressionist treatments of the theme the idea, implicit or explicit that somehow a New Man would emerge from the holocaust. Many Expressionist plays are *Läuterungsdramen*, i.e. plays of purification, and the constantly repeated demand of the Expressionist programmes for the "regeneration of mankind" is closely tied to the progress of the war. As has been seen the wave of enthusiasm which had generally characterised the first two years of the war was followed by a steadily mounting wave of criticism and open rebellion against the war, which culminated in active pacifism. The final stage seemed to have been reached after the war when Ernst Toller (1893-1939) presented *his* drama of the man to emerge from the war—*The German Hinkemann* (1921-22). Generally speaking Expressionist dramas are not tragedies, they are optimistic at heart. They tend to be fashioned after the model of Strindberg's *Way to Damascus* and show the stations along the way to be taken out of the old world into a new and brighter future. Toller's play, however, is explicitly described as a tragedy. The form still follows the path taken by the German soldier emerging from the war but now there is no upward climb to a new dawn, instead the end is disaster and the final words of the play reiterate the motif of the impending End of the World. Although Toller's work follows the favourite Expressionist pattern of the *Stationendrama* making the whole into a modern mystery play round the figure of the crucified Hinkemann, nevertheless, despite this epic form Toller has constructed a very well made and extremely compact tragedy in three acts modelled in part on Büchner's famous *Woyzeck* which also took as its his hero or anti-hero a poor soldier rendered impotent and crushed by a brutal and calculating military machine. There is a clear line of development from *Woyzeck* through Brecht's *Drums in the Night* to Toller's *Hinkemann* and Borcherdt's *The Man Outside* written after the end of the Second World War. The drama of the returned soldier has in fact become almost an integral part of German theatrical history, and even the castration theme here associated with it is not so unusual in German literature. The *Storm and Stress* dramatist Lenz used it in his *Hofmeister* which Brecht later adapted and Brecht himself exploited the theme in his *Man is a Man*. That it is not a specifically Germanic theme was demonstrated by Hemingway who afflicted the hero of his *Fiesta* in the same way.

It is sometimes assumed that because of the working-class setting Toller's tragedy marks a move away from Expressionist drama towards post-war "new objectivity" and disillusionment. This is only partly true, for the play is certainly not intended as a naturalistic portrayal of post-war reality. Even the setting is Expressionistic— only the barest essence or abstract of the working-class milieu is shown and Hinkemann himself is clearly marked out as the

Expressionist seeker after truth by his manner of speaking which is described as having "the ponderous groping quality of the elemental soul". Typically Expressionistic too is the treatment of the theme of love both in the physical and the spiritual sense. And where Hasenclever's *Antigone* demanded a vast arena Toller now moves to the circus or rather the ambience of the travelling side-show which Brecht was also later to exploit so effectively. Apart from the attractions of its lively demotic speech this milieu demonstrates the emptiness of post-war living when "royalty, top-brass, priests and show-men" give the people what they want, namely *Rausch*, intoxication, hysteria induced by false and brutalising spectacles. It is the sight of the degradation Hinkemann is forced to accept for her sake which opens Greta's eyes. The distant ideal of the rich, exciting life proves worthless, dirty and not worth reaching out for. The nature of life, the problem of human happiness, the quest for "truth" and "purpose"—all basic Expressionistic themes—are discussed by Hinkemann in his question-and-answer game with the party functionary and it is clear that the former revolutionary Toller no longer feels so optimistic about finding any simple political or social solution to them. However, the quest for truth is pursued through all levels of discourse from the stupid workers' quarrel which clearly unmasks all facile slogans, through fair-ground jargon to the long subjective monologue in which Hinkemann in slightly veiled language tells the story of his personal tragedy, coming finally to ecstatic utterance, at first awkward as Hinkemann gropes for words but in the end with "the overwhelming power of great simplicity" culminating in verse.

Far from being a naturalistic working-class tragedy Toller's play is an Expressionistic vision. Not only Greta's eyes are opened, Hinkemann himself is vouchsafed a vision of the truth:

> Now I can see all the way! Right to the naked heart. I see what men are. I see the age we live in! Sir . . . the war's on again! Men are murdering each other and laughing. *Men are murdering each other and laughing!*

This is the true visionary insight. The end of the war does not mean the end of the war. Man's inhumanity to man continues and ridicule and cynicism are its strongest weapons. The post-war jazz age is a hectic period of ruthless competition in all spheres from party politics to big business and devil take the hindmost. Hinkemann who does not even have the protection of a returned soldiers' organisation collapses completely in this world of newspaper sensations, anti-semitism, prostitutes, stuffed-shirts and rubber coshes. But it is he, the outsider who sees the world as it really is:

> You walk along the streets, day after day, like a blind man. And then all of a sudden you *see*. Max, what you see is terrible. You see souls. And do you know what souls look like? Not like any living thing. One soul is a bull-neck, the next a love machine, the third a cash register, the fourth a military organisation, the fifth a rubber cosh . . . Did you ever poke a little bird's eyes out?

But ridicule is the worst crime, laughing when a poor soul writhes in suffering, raw with pain. Greta, he discovers, has not laughed at him, but by this time there is nowhere for her, she is a hunted animal in the jungle of life, caught like Hinkemann in a net from which there is apparently no escape other than the one she chooses —suicide.

What then is the message of the play? Is it one of resignation and despair as the final words, conjuring up yet again the Expressionist image of the End of the World seem to suggest? No, there is more light than this and the "tragedy" is despite everything basically optimistic. There is no need for the murdering to continue, no need for the people to obey orders and kill each other. People stone the spirit, mock it, abuse life, crucify it . . . But it does not have to be this way if people would open their eyes, see the world as it really is and accept the message of love for common humanity. It is easy to laugh at this and deride the rather naïve political idealism which inspires it. But, as Toller himself clearly saw, cynicism is no solution. War is an evil which must be combatted with all means available. The medium he and his fellow Expressionists adopted to combat the menace of war was the theatre for which they produced these tremendously powerful plays.

J.M.R.

H. F. Garten:
Modern German Drama (London 1959)

Walter Gropius ed.:
The Theater of the Bauhaus (Wesleyan University Press, 1961)

M. Hamburger & C. Middleton eds.:
Modern German Poetry 1910-1960 (London, 1963)

Claude Hill & Ralph Ley:
The Drama of German Expressionism. A German-English Bibliography (University of North Carolina Press, 1960)

Egbert Krispyn:
Style and Society in German Literary Expressionism (University of Florida, 1964)

Hector Maclean:
'Expressionism' in *Periods of German Literature* ed. J. M. Ritchie (London, 1966)

J. M. Ritchie:
German Theatre between the Wars and the Genteel Tradition, *Modern Drama*, Feb. 1965; The Expressionist Revival, *Seminar* Spring, 1966

R. H. Samuel & R. Hinton Thomas:
Expressionism in German Life, Literature and The Theatre, 1910-1924 (Cambridge, 1939)

Walter H. Sokel:
The Writer in Extremis: Expressionism in 20th Century German Literature (Stanford, California, 1959)
An Anthology of German Expressionist Drama, a prelude to the absurd (Doubleday Anchor, A365)

August Strindberg:
Eight Expressionist Plays (Bantam Classics, QC 261)

WAR

A Te Deum

Carl Hauptmann

1913

Translated by J. M. Ritchie

WAR, A Te Deum

Dramatis Personae

PRINCE KAIL, *Minister of State*

PRINCESS KAIL

ENOCH, *their son*

GRUTSCHKA

MATER MARIA SALESI

A SECOND MINISTER

SCHALAST, *confidential clerk to the Minister*

APTEKA, *a rentier*

OTREMBA, *a rentier*

THE PORTER

CASPAR, *a servant*

PETRUS HEISSLER

FRAU HEISSLER

THE EUROPEAN RECKONER

THE ARCHANGEL IN ARMOUR

THE GREAT POWER BEASTS

THE THREE MONSTROUS FIGURES

A DRUNK

A WRETCHED WOMAN

ANOTHER WRETCHED WOMAN

A MISERABLE MAN

THE ESCAPED VISIONARY

A FRENCH GENERAL

A SECOND GENERAL

A BUTLER

TWO NAPOLEONIC GRENADIER GUARDS

A FRENCH LEADER

A SECOND LEADER

A RAGGED WOMAN

A VIVANDIERE

A CHILD

A GROUP OF ANXIOUS RAGGED WOMEN

A GROUP OF NURSES

FATHER FRANCIS

A HAIRY CRIPPLE

ANOTHER CRIPPLE

A THIRD CRIPPLE

A ONE–EYED, ONE–ARMED CRIPPLE

ANOTHER CRIPPLE (*Shepherd*)

THE CRIPPLE (*Philosopher*)

THE CRIPPLE (*Smith*)

A CRIPPLE (*in tail-coat*)

A MERRY CRIPPLE

Ministers, Brass-hats, Gentlemen of High Society, young couples, young officers, ladies in balldresses, servants, bearers, poor people, children, a group of rentiers, a group of factory girls and village maidens, miners and other workers, a column of German conscripts, a German infantry column in close formation, French officers, French soldiers, wounded of various nationalities, individual nursing sisters, a nonagenarian, German troops, corpses, creatures variously crippled and vilely clad.

PART ONE

On one side the palace with the park behind a mighty iron railing and tall hedges. The terrace with cane chairs and tables. The parapets of the terrace rich with flowers. On the other side low village huts. Between them runs the village street. Entrances from various quarters.

There is an evening reception in the palace. Two torches on the gate-posts. The terrace is not particularly well lit. The windows of the palace on the other hand are ablaze with light from within. Round the iron railing stand poor people, mainly women and children. But a few menfolk too. Across the road in the village there is light in one window only. Violin music for dancing can be heard from the palace. A few village children and girls dance to the music outside the gates.

PRINCESS KAIL: *wrapped from head to foot in a red silk shawl, hair parted severely, comes out of the palace, descends the steps into the garden and calls softly]* Enoch . . . Enoch . . . my son . . . the red dawn of battle is beginning to break . . . crimson colours burn before my eyes, oh they fill me with rapture . . . Enoch where are you . . .

ENOCH KAIL: *a young officer of the Black Hussars, appears on an upper balcony of the palace]* I am up here, mother . . . why do you call . . . what place have I at your feast of rejoicing?

PRINCESS KAIL: *hurries over to a bush]* I must break off a twig of withered leaf . . . and smell decay and death . . . I feel again now we are all sacrificed . . . I too roam around aimlessly . . . find no rest in this house of rejoicing . . . visions enrapture me . . . I see hosts of white and red assassins storming against each other . . . over our fields and meadows . . . I see Death in a thousand bright guises rage and strike as with invisible hammers . . . it crushes all with its mighty juggernaut . . . and I must listen to the choruses of war which thunder in the air, like the consorts of armoured angels . . .

ENOCH KAIL: Mother . . . come to your senses . . .

PRINCESS KAIL: *as if awakening]* The sublime is silent now . . . oh . . . I have you again . . . I was alarmed . . . I see you again . . .

26

ENOCH KAIL: Mother . . . your eyes are radiant . . .

PRINCESS KAIL: Come and join the revellers, Enoch . . . appear gay, even if you are not . . . come, before father or the guests start to look for us.

ENOCH KAIL: Today I have no further desire to appear before my father. I am filthy and besmirched . . . to you alone I can always confess . . . for you are my mother . . . a mother always delights in kissing away the marks of shame from the bodies of her children.

PRINCESS KAIL: Yes . . . yes . . . yes . . .

ENOCH KAIL: But father's eye pierces me as with sharp thorns so that I needs must be ashamed . . . ah . . . yet more visitors now at midnight . . .

[*he has disappeared from the balcony. On one side-path a solemn procession of servants and uniformed dignitaries, accompanying a sedan-chair. They approach silently*].

PRINCESS KAIL: *looks about her timidly, as though to herself*] More guests . . . now at midnight . . . Enoch . . . Enoch.

A fat uniformed Porter has suddenly appeared at the gates and opened them. The Princess hastens into the palace.
The people at the railings, as the sedan-chair proceeds through the palace gates:

Hurrah . . . hurrah . . . hurrah . . .

Flunkeys from the palace leap onto the steps of the entrance. The sedan-chair is carried forward to it. Out of the palace doors stream Gentlemen of High Society, Out of the sedan-chair climbs a Bear in an ermine cloak, who marches solemn and erect into the palace, greeted on all sides by deep bows and reverences. Accompanied by Gentlemen and flunkeys. It all takes place in utter silence. The terrace is empty once more. As the doors of the palace close again, the Russian National Anthem and a fanfare ring out for a moment. Meanwhile the porter pushes back the surging populace at the gates.

PORTER: Keep calm . . . if you lot don't keep calm . . . you there at the other side of the railings . . . I'll have to chase you away altogether.

A WRETCHED WOMAN: Mr. Porter . . . Mr. Porter . . .

PORTER: What is it then . . . what do you want with Mr. Porter . . .

WOMAN: I think it must be our Gracious Lady's birthday today . . . there is a ball. It must be a birthday party today.

PORTER: Yes, yes . . . quite right . . . there's a birthday party today . . . Her Excellency the Princess, saw the light of day for the first time on this very date . . .

ANOTHER WRETCHED-LOOKING WOMAN: Look, they're bringing somebody else in a sedan-chair . . .

On another side-path another solemn procession of liveried lackeys, and uniformed dignitaries appears accompanying a sedan-chair. They approach the palace silently. The people at the railing shout:

Hurrah . . . hurrah . . . hurrah . . .

Flunkeys from the palace leap to the steps. The sedan-chair is carried forward. Out of castle doors stream Gentlemen of High Society. Some Gentlemen in diplomatic and military uniform too. Out of the sedan-chair climbs a Cock in an ermine cloak, who marches solemn and erect into the palace, greeted on all sides by deep bows and compliments. Accompanied by Gentlemen and Servants. It all takes place in utter silence. The terrace is empty once more. As the palace doors close again, the 'Marseillaise' and a fanfare ring out for a moment. The miserable people at the railing try to join in the 'Marseillaise'.

PORTER: Have you all gone absolutely mad . . . shut up will you . . . I'll drive you right off the street and back into your miserable huts. Insolent rabble.

WRETCHED WOMAN: Mr. Porter . . . Mr. Porter . . .

PORTER: Well, what is it? . . . What do you want with Mr. Porter?

WRETCHED WOMAN: But I thought it was our Gracious Lady the Princess's birthday today . . .

PORTER: Quite right, quite right . . . God knows it is . . . but the whole affair is beginning to look a bit different . . . after all it's midnight now . . . and sometimes things happen in the world, nobody has foreseen . . . something's stirring . . .

make room . . . I don't know what's going on any more . . . there's another visitor arriving.

WRETCHED WOMAN: Jesus . . . Jesus . . . another sedan-chair . . . what secrets are these?

A WRETCHED MAN: *at the railings*] Is there a cock or a bear in it, I wonder . . .

On another side-path another solemn procession of liveried lackeys and uniformed dignitaries appears, accompanying a sedan-chair. They approach the palace silently. The people at the railing shout:

Hurrah . . . hurrah . . . hurrah . . .

Flunkeys from the palace leap to the steps. The sedan-chair is carried forward. Out of the palace doors stream Gentlemen of High Society. Some Gentlemen in diplomatic and military uniform too. Out of the sedan-chair climbs an Eagle in an ermine cloak, who marches solemn and erect, into the palace, greeted on all sides by deep bows and reverences. Accompanied by Gentlemen and Servants.

It all takes place in utter silence. The terrace is empty once more. As the palace doors close again, 'Heil dir im Siegerkranze' or 'Deutschland, Deutschland' and a fanfare ring out for a moment. The people at the railing try to join in . . .

PORTER: Dead silence there!

VARIOUS VOICES: *from the people*] Mr. Porter . . . Mr. Porter . . .

PORTER: Yes, yes, yes, Mr. Porter, Mr. Porter, you'll be the death of him yet, it may have been the birthday of our Gracious Lady in the palace today . . . and the anniversary of the death of Tom, Dick or Harry . . . and the Feast Day of Peter and Paul . . . and the execution day of a hundred common murderers . . . and the Remembrance Day of various highly decorated Gentlemen . . . but right now I can give you no further explanation of what is going on . . . ye gods and little fishes . . . it's enough to make your eyes pop, and your ears grow wings . . . why there's another procession of sedan-chairs arriving . . . it's going to be a real midnight turn-out.

The People at the Railing shout:

Hurrah . . . hurrah . . . hurrah . . .

A whole procession of sedan-chairs arrives. Again surrounded by liveried flunkeys and uniformed dignitaries. Lackeys rush out of the palace. The Gentlemen stream forth anew. The sedan-chairs are carried to the entrance stairway one after the other. From the first a Wolf climbs out. Another sedan-chair. Other animals climb out. Each in ermine cloak. Cries of Hurrah again from the crowd. Constant bowing and exchange of elaborate greetings. Each animal marches solemnly into the palace. Some National Anthem or other sounds out. Until the last sedan-chair is empty—from it an erect Whale has stepped forth. And amidst the bowing etc. and shouts from the crowd, the terrace has become empty once more and lies in semi-darkness. As the doors close 'God Save the Queen' rings out and a fanfare.

PRINCE KAIL: *appears from the palace door]* Porter . . . lock the gates . . .

PORTER: Very good, Your Excellency.

KAIL: We are having an important conference, Porter . . . so let no unauthorised person in . . . dead or alive . . . hahahaha . . . of course, you couldn't just grab the dead by the throat and . . . throw them out again, even if they did come . . .

Goes back into the palace. Off.

PORTER: *approaching the open gates]* Well . . . this is a pretty pass.

He goes rigid, the great bunch of keys in his hand, his face registers horror. A new sedan-chair arrives. Completely ghostly, silent. The iron gates open of their own accord. Liveried lackeys and dignitaries. But the faces—death-heads. All are wearing Polish uniforms. Moving through the gates and up the steps in complete silence. No welcoming party of any kind appears. From the sedan-chair climbs a Being enveloped in ermine with the bony skull of a beast of prey, glides silently up the steps and disappears into the palace, the palace door opening silently of its own accord before them. Flunkeys and dignitaries and sedan-chair disappear in complete silence like ghosts.

When the PORTER eventually pulls himself together out of his stupor, all sorts of young couples, Ladies and Gentlemen of society, young officers with elegant partners on their arm are fleeing silently like shadows out of the house.

ALL: *whispering confusedly*] These are serious times that have suddenly come upon us.

THE PEOPLE: *flee too joining those of High Society. In complete silence. Also whispering confusedly*] These are serious times that have suddenly come upon us . . . These are serious times that have suddenly come upon us . . .

MINISTER KAIL: *appears laughing fearfully. Just at this moment* PETRUS HEISSLER *has opened his window which is brightly lit from within and has stuck his careworn, enormous head out the window*] Ha . . . what on earth . . . what uncanny face is that, for heaven's sake!

PORTER: It is the prophet of doom and disaster, Your Excellency . . . the miner Petrus Heissler . . . he is just looking up at the night sky . . . to observe the comet which appeared in the sky to-night.

KAIL: What . . . a comet . . . where . . . one never even gets time to take a look up at the night sky nowadays . . .

PORTER: Up there . . . there it is . . . you can see it with the naked eye . . .

SECOND MINISTER: *enters hurriedly*] There is still somebody missing, Your Excellency, otherwise the conference could begin immediately . . . The Great Powers are all assembled . . . to a man . . .

KAIL: Of course, of course, my dear colleague . . . still somebody missing . . . but listen my dear colleague . . . take a look up at the sky . . . there's even a comet in the sky, unfortunately it is not written in the stars . . .

SECOND MINISTER: I must confess I am exceedingly happy that we've managed to bring all the Great Powers together round the conference table so willing and peaceful . . . and that they are just yawning at each other for the time being . . . and now and again winking to each other and smiling politely.

KAIL: *while both go back to the door*] Yes . . . my God . . . dear colleague . . . there *is* somebody missing . . . why, the main actor is still missing . . . just what are we going to do if this somebody doesn't come . . . [*both off*]

Deep silence reigns over the palace. The torches on the pillars at the gates burn down lower. One goes out. The terrace is empty and dark.

PORTER: *leans as if dreaming at the gates and looks up to the stars*] Unfortunately it is not written in the stars . . .

Meanwhile another sedan-chair approaches in the dark. It looks like a lantern lit from within. It is carried by two workmen. Before the locked gates a high-pitched voice calls from the sedan-chair 'Open up . . . Open up . . . the famous EUROPEAN RECKONER *is coming . . . The Great Powers are already waiting for him' . . . the* PORTER *gives a start and opens mechanically. The sedan-chair is carried to the foot of the steps. The* EUROPEAN RECKONER *gets out. A withered little mannikin. Very lean, with grotesquely-furrowed face. In a yellow, very narrowly-cut frock-coat. Very pointed, black satin pumps, black satin trousers. He is carrying a lantern in his hand and has a globe of the world under his arm. Smiling craftily he has leapt out of the chair as quick as a flash and looks as quick and slippery as quicksilver.*

EUROPEAN RECKONER: You see, the Great Powers are all assembled already . . . hehehehe . . . I'm coming . . . I'm coming . . . I'm urgently needed here . . . you can believe me . . . urgently needed . . . you can bet your life I am . . . well now . . . and who, may I ask, are you, my good man . . .

PORTER: His Highness the Prince of Kail and Minister of State's Head Porter.

EUROPEAN RECKONER: Yes, yes, yes . . . up the steps quickly . . . I have everything I need here with me. I'm urgently needed in there . . . for you see in there sits Black versus White . . . the Gospel versus The Koran . . . you know for yourself what that means, don't you? The Slave Race against the Master Race . . . the cavalry man against the trader with the pack on his back . . . the people who plough the land . . . against the people who plough the sea . . . my dear porter . . . they would all be at each other's throats, until the last gasp was squeezed out like the last wheeze out of the bagpipes . . . hehehehehe . . .

He disappears with crafty smile, tripping into the palace. The PORTER *closes the gates after him and listens. A surge of noise wells out as soon as the* EUROPEAN RECKONER *steps in.*

A YOUNG JEWESS: *comes skipping along the village street. When she sees the lighted window in the village hut, she stares in for a while. Then she hurries on to the park gates and rattles them. When nobody appears, she runs quickly along the railings*] Porter . . . Porter . . . open up . . . open up . . .

PORTER: *comes, taking his time*] Open up? No question of that Miss . . . I can't let you in tonight . . . certainly not to our gracious young master.

ENOCH KAIL: *has suddenly stepped out through the French windows and calls down from the balcony*] Gruschka . . . darling . . . [*he disappears hurriedly*].

PORTER: *intimidated*] Oh, our gracious young master himself.

ENOCH KAIL: *appears out of a side door of the palace. Brusquely to the Porter*] Now then . . . get a move on won't you and open that gate . . . and then clear out . . . there's nothing more you need to overhear . . . understand . . . you fat hypocrite and slanderer and eye-roller—and be sure you really close your ground floor window . . . that's my advice . . . otherwise you'll get a few rocks round your head . . . and sand in your eyes . . .

The PORTER *has opened the gate, left it open and disappears round the back of the palace, without daring to say a word.*

ENOCH: Gruschka . . . darling . . . you've been running . . . in your condition . . . what's wrong . . . what's the matter . . .

GRUSCHKA: Enoch . . . I have seen a vision . . .

ENOCH: Darling, you can hardly breathe . . . yet your eyes are laughing . . .

GRUSCHKA: I know quite well that you probably spend your time paying court to God knows how many noble young ladies . . . and you've only let poor Gruschka into your bedroom as a passing plaything to dwell with her in Paradise . . . clarion-calls . . . in the blood . . . or from somewhere or other . . . everybody can feel harsh orders in the blood already hear them echo in their ears . . . yes, you . . . are a scoundrel . . . a sinner [*suddenly tender and sad*] Oh, Enoch . . . you have been forging cheques in your father's name again . . . why have you again squandered so much of your father's money . . .

ENOCH: *timidly*] What do you know about that, my darling . . .

GRUSCHKA: The stories are already going the rounds like a malicious whisper.

ENOCH: *still more timidly*] And you don't despise me for it, my darling . . .

GRUSCHKA: Oh . . . I have heard the trumpets of the Archangels in the air . . . now you will have to gird yourself for quite different deeds and crimes . . .

ENOCH: *eyes downcast*] Yes . . . the muscles of my body can become taut, because I am ruthless, capable of great deeds . . . and of living boldly . . . man has but one irresistible impulse . . . to feel and enjoy life to the full . . . he lives on this earth, after all . . . and not in the cloister . . . what is wealth for . . . but I was supposed merely to put out a cloud of words . . . perform my deeds in books and newspapers . . . in words . . . live an empty shadow of a life . . . instead of madness, fullness of feelings . . . and I will not let myself be gagged by frustrated desires . . . I won't let myself be made into a tame ballroom gigolo or reduced to a polite, glib lip-juggler . . . I see no other purpose in life, but to risk myself and my life and to squander . . .

GRUSCHKA: *strokes him soothingly*] Little beads of perspiration are breaking out on your forehead for very shame . . . you are trying to defend your misdeeds . . . don't look for reasons for your sins . . . oh, Enoch . . . it's not because you kiss my feet when they are naked . . . or because you are noble and rich . . . and my father only a poor village shopkeeper . . . he would strike me dead if he caught me . . . 'Though the earth be full of filth'—says my father 'Yet heaven is as pure as snow . . . and pure as heaven is my Gruschka'—let my father speak as his years see things . . . I will still cast body and soul at your feet . . . Enoch . . .

ENOCH: Where are you leading me, darling . . .

GRUSCHKA: There, to the window . . .

ENOCH: *stepping forwards with her briskly*] What do you expect to find there?

GRUSCHKA: *as they approach* PETRUS HEISSLER'S *window, going on tip-toe*] Softly now . . . I want to show you a man . . . who prays . . .

ENOCH: Hahaha . . . [*with muted voice*] a man who prays? . . .

[*his face assumes an expression of astonishment as they both stare into the lighted window*] Not a man who prays . . . but one who has a very strange visitor . . .

GRUSCHKA: Enoch . . . [*she clings to him*] Describe to me what you see . . . because otherwise I might think I'm imagining what I see . . .

ENOCH: *still staring fixedly into the window*] No . . . you're not just imagining . . . Gruschka . . . I see it just as clearly as you do . . . with enraptured eyes . . . I see an Archangel in armour sitting there, leaning his arm on the poor wooden table before Petrus Heissler . . . and speaking forceful words to the careworn, powerful old man . . .

GRUSCHKA: Can you understand the words, Enoch? . . .

ENOCH: No, I cannot understand the words. I can only see that the prophet of doom has laughter lighting up all his features like an astonished child . . . and that his great grey eyes are filled with a misty gleaming . . .

GRUSCHKA: Then you see and feel it all as I do . . . can you also see that the angel in armour has a sharp sword at his side . . .

ENOCH: Yes, I can see that too . . . indeed yes.

GRUSCHKA: *has suddenly pulled* ENOCH *back to the street a little. There she kneels down*] I love my mother and father . . . I love my brothers and my sisters . . . I love the dear departed . . . I am prepared to have my fingers chopped off for my brothers and sisters . . . and arms and hands for my father and mother . . . I am prepared to leap into the fire for my God . . . but for you, Enoch, [*she has leapt to her feet again*] I am ready to sing songs and dance in the fire . . . for you I am ready to hold up my heart in my hands . . . that drop after drop may flow out with groans of bliss. Oh, Enoch . . . I love you as I do no other thing upon this earth. Why? because you revolt against the insipid and self-satisfied in life. [*She kisses him, embraces him, lets him go again, scurries away a few steps, points to the sky*] The tailed star goes through space . . . now hard deeds and crimes of quite a different order will mature in your blood . . . when the mighty Archangels blow the trumpet. [*In the palace loud strife can be heard. Two French windows are flung open. The Bear looks out of one of them, the Cock out of the other*] Yes, yes, yes . . . lets have some fresh air . . . fresh air at last . . .

VOICES: *from within in violent strife. Various voices heard in a confusion of shouts*] What's the point of all these calculations . . . if all the advantages don't end up in my lap . . . we are not human beings, you know, you've got to appreciate that we are POWERS . . . we are the GREAT POWERS after all . . . hahahaha . . . ridiculous . . . Borders of ink and paper . . . Borders of wood . . . Borders of steel . . . all such borders keeping Great Powers apart are fragile . . . [*the palace door opens.* MINISTERS *and* BRASS-HATS *come out*]

EUROPEAN RECKONER: *also rushing out, demonstrates with the Globe*] Yes, my dear Ministers of State . . . and High Dignitaries . . . it is very simple to demonstrate . . . here is the WORLD . . . agreed . . . naturally the whole world should be Russian . . . hehehehe . . . but it isn't yet no, it isn't yet . . . and of course, the European Reckoner has to be tolerant and be able to assume a different point of view . . . agreed . . . so this is the WORLD . . . and the whole world should be French too . . . but it isn't yet . . . no . . . it isn't yet . . . it would be very pleasant . . . for example, the French publishers could cover the whole world with their books—the French armaments manufacturers could equip the whole world with their weapons . . . not weapons of war, of course . . . just mutually autonomous weapons . . . hehehehe . . . or the whole world should really be Italian . . . or I even think it ought to be Austrian . . . no . . . it should be German . . . but most of all it should be English . . . for what the Great Powers want . . . you see . . . my High Dignitaries . . . what could Great Powers want but the whole world . . . that's what they want, you see . . . that's what they want.

MINISTER KAIL: *appears on the terrace from inside*] Do come back inside, Gentlemen . . . the Conference is continuing . . . the room has cooled down . . . tempers too are completely calm again. [*All off*]

ENOCH KAIL: *who had fled into the bushes with* GRUSCHKA, *creeping forward again*] Do you understand . . . what is going on here?

GRUSCHKA: Hahahaha . . . what is it . . . what kind of animals were those looking out of the windows . . .

ENOCH: Come . . . we can peep through the curtains . . .

GRUSCHKA: *peeping in*] Enoch . . . there are no men round the green table!

ENOCH: No, God preserve us . . . it's the Bear . . . the Wolf . . . the Lion . . . the Cock . . . the Eagle . . . the Whale . . . all merciless forces . . . even skulls of beasts of prey, which are even more voracious than the beasts . . . they are all the Great Powers . . . and that little pipecleaner fellow, the European Reckoner, is pouring words out in front of them like a waterfall . . .

GRUSCHKA: Nothing but figures . . . he is speaking in figures . . . *The doors are flung open again from within.* MINISTERS *and* HIGH DIGNITARIES *stream out again. All talking at once.* ENOCH *and* GRUSCHKA *disappear:* No, no, no . . . that's no solution. . . never come to the end of it that way . . . you've just got to accept the fact that between Asia and Europe there is simply no place for a Poland . . .

EUROPEAN RECKONER: *uses the globe to demonstrate*] Hehehehe . . . my most respected and honourable Great Powers . . . I admit it entirely without reservation . . . a serious error was allowed to slip in right at the very beginning in the arrangement of this our stony world . . . this error is the infamous growing together of countries and continents . . . yes . . . gentlemen, if Poland for example still existed as a mighty dam against Asia . . . you see . . . hehehehe . . . Europe and Asia . . . why they are the Siamese twins . . . I am sure every one of us Europeans would wish today that they could be surgically separated . . . for there is no question, is there? Europe would be an Eldorado, if, for example, one could separate it by an ocean from Asia . . . listen . . . gentlemen . . . a sea between Europe and Asia . . . and the Bear would be back on the other side of the great water again . . . and we in Europe would be alone again . . . we could fight over advantages AMONG OURSELVES . . . hehehehehe . . . a sea . . . even a European Reckoner cannot create a sea out of the bleak plains at this late date . . . so we must try to even out this earthly error . . . reduce it intelligently to terms of human profit . . .

He becomes lost in thought over the globe.

MINISTER KAIL: *comes hurrying out of the palace*] Do come back in again, Gentlemen . . . some mutually advantageous solution must be found at all costs . . . after all we're not trying to settle all our differences at once and for all eternity, are we?

[*All drift back again*] . . . *Only the*

EUROPEAN RECKONER: *still stands for a while lost in contemplation of the globe and talks on, as though not noticing that there is nobody near him*] My dear sirs . . . it is certainly true that a whole series of so-called Great Powers exist on our earth . . . which all want to assert themselves . . . the greater the Power, the more this is so . . . but there is certainly no Great Power which has yet proved itself conclusively superior to economic advantage . . . I have my fine scales for each of you Great Powers to see . . . I weigh and weigh . . . I shall now weigh out every grain of possible advantage for each of you . . . hehehehehe . . . because that's what the European Reckoner is for . . .

Along the village street strides a lone ARCHANGEL, *marches in through the gates.*

EUROPEAN RECKONER: *suddenly as if mesmerised*] Ah . . . Ah . . . [*plunges his hand through his hair convulsively. Lets the globe fall. Stares fixedly at the approaching* ARCHANGEL] A Higher Power is coming . . . I must get out of here . . . help . . . hehehe . . . help; a Higher Power is coming . . . hehehehe . . . I cannot move from this spot.

The ARCHANGEL *marches up the steps.*

EUROPEAN RECKONER: *curls up into a ball, laughing to himself*] I cannot move from this spot . . . hehehehe.

The ARCHANGEL *strikes down the* EUROPEAN RECKONER *with his sword, so that his corpse falls onto the steps. Immediately all lights disappear. So too all noise from within. Deathly silence and darkness. The* ARCHANGEL *alone bathed in light turns back and with swinging strides retraces his steps and disappears. And now there is only* HEISSLER'S *window gradually visible as splash of brightness. Till all sinks into deep darkness again.*

PART TWO

*Dawn comes out of the deep darkness. Palace and park stretch out quite
empty. In the village there is light burning now in some huts. An*
ARCHANGEL *in armour steps out of* PETRUS HEISSLER'S *door. Behind
him the old prophet of doom himself.*

ARCHANGEL: *turning round to talk to him*] I want to make use of your
yearning soul, Petrus Heissler . . . you are to be the mes-
senger . . .

PETRUS HEISSLER: *careworn and brooding, holding an ancient holy book
open in his hand*] What tidings shall I bring to mankind, sire . . .

ARCHANGEL: WAR . . . proclaim it with your voice of doom
. . . let mankind tremble and weep . . . WAR will reap the
harvest . . . till death grins from mutilated bodies in the fields
and streets and in the dwellings of man . . . till father and
mother . . . brother and sister . . . parents and children . . .
friend and friend . . . and the lover and the beloved can no
longer find each other, except among the dead . . .

PETRUS HEISSLER: War, sire . . . is that what I have to proclaim?

ARCHANGEL: Proclaim war . . . this will revitalize the tamed
forces of animality on earth, so that they fall upon each other
. . . murderous armies against murderous armies . . . and
nowhere a place remains, where a lamb may safely graze . . .
only armed men everywhere . . . only thieving and murderous
men in whose hand and in whose eye there is death for their
neighbour . . .

PETRUS HEISSLER: With my voice of doom, I am to proclaim war,
because you bid me do so . . .

ARCHANGEL: Oh, Petrus Heissler . . . you duped worshipper . . .
you imagined there were only roses in the lap of God . . . the
sweet fragrance of the mountains of home for heart and eye . . .
You saw His Heavens like this—you fancied the morning sun
—God's golden fire—there but to ripen vine and olive and
wheat . . . and to make the blood of men heavy with love
. . . proclaim war, in God's name, Petrus Heissler—God is

39

crueller than the forces of animality . . . even if millions die, milliards awake anew out of His death . . . fear not, Petrus Heissler . . . tremble not before the infinite. God is empty as the depths of the ether . . . and boundless as the immeasurable sky . . . God is the great incendiary, who makes the belly of the mountains into fiery cauldrons, that gigantic rock masses spiral high up into the blue ether and mountains of ruins crash down into the valleys and bury puny mankind . . . proclaim war, Petrus Heissler . . . God is a dark name . . . God is the ultimate mystery . . . only weaklings want to reduce God to human form . . . want to carry him around in their pocket . . . hahahaha . . . on one side the pocket mirror, to admire themselves in secret . . . on the other side, God . . . so that He will be sure to guide their beloved ego to prosperity and comfort . . . no, no, Petrus Heissler . . . God wants to measure out the limits of eternity . . . God wants to go further . . . God wants to cast himself upon us like seed . . .

PETRUS HEISSLER: *tries to say something but he recoils once more, then summons innermost resources, to say*] God is a hand, which stretches out towards me from on high . . . it wants to raise me up out of bestiality, it wants to snatch me up into the light.

ARCHANGEL: Blessed be he who sees the hand . . . but God's body is still a cloud of scurrying grey mist . . . the awful screaming emptiness . . . a myriad vortex of men slaying each other . . . and even you too are still only a mortal sacrifice and must sow yourself into the furrow holding the vision in your fading eye . . .

A DRUNK: *comes from the back along the street, he bawls*] 'Valleri . . . vallera . . . zu Augsburg im Goldenen Stern . . . Hat mich die Kellnerin so gern' . . . Leave me in peace . . . hahahaha don't trouble me with Dukes and Princes . . . with Ministers and Police . . . what has it got to do with the police anyway if I drink the starvation wage I get . . . I'm over twenty-one . . . hahahahaha . . . I'm a free man, aren't I . . . and if I want to sleep in a ditch once in a while . . . instead of with that nagging old woman . . . 'Valleri . . . vallera . . . zu Augsburg im Goldenen Stern . . . Hat mich die Kellnerin so gern' . . .

He staggers with forced sobriety into a hut.

PETRUS HEISSLER: *lost in self-probing, running one hand through his hair agitatedly and holding the book in the other, taking no notice of* THE DRUNK *who has now disappeared*] My voice is hoarse . . . I am an old miner . . . for years I have lain on my back deep down in the belly of the earth . . . stark naked and dripping with sweat . . . lonely hour after lonely hour . . . in the pitch dark . . . in the light of the guttering little oil lamp . . . always silent . . . With no word crossing my lips among the eternal, monotonous blows of the pick . . . with all that my voice is long since hard and dried up, sire . . . and mine is only *one* voice . . .

A scream from the house into which THE DRUNK *disappeared.*

A MALE VOICE: *rings out clearly through it*] I'll kill you, woman . . . I'll kill you . . . try to push me away from your bed would you . . . hit me in the face with a poker would you? You old rag-bag of bones with the chattering chin . . . dare to despise me would you?

CHILDREN: *come out of the house with screams of terror*] Father . . . you're strangling mother . . . father . . . father's an animal. Father . . . you're strangling mother . . . [*Shouts from inside too and the children rush back in again*]. God help us . . . God help us—you're strangling mother . . . if you don't let . . . let go—let her go, will you . . . she is going blue . . . she's getting blue in the face . . . Help . . . help . . . help.

PETRUS HEISSLER: *in sudden upsurge of rage*] Sire . . . won't you bring help—that monster is murdering his wife . . . that monster is murdering his wife . . .

PETRUS HEISSLER *rushes back into his own hut and reappears armed with a crowbar, but the* ARCHANGEL *holds him in an iron grip.*

CHILDREN VOICES: *screaming from the house again*] Mother . . . mother . . . mother's dead . . . mother's dead . . . mother's dead . . . and father, the beast, has fallen asleep with his head on the table . . . help . . . help . . .

A CROWD OF VILLAGE AND FACTORY GIRLS: *wander past singing*]

B*

Sunday is the day of joy
When I go walking with my boy,
Tirra—birra, Fee Fi Fo,
I'm his Annie; he's my Joe. [*Off*]

The ARCHANGEL *has meanwhile disappeared,* PETRUS HEISSLER *stands alone, the crowbar in his hand still, rubbing his eyes as if he were only now waking up completely.*

MRS. HEISSLER: *from inside*] Husband . . . restless spirit . . . where have you got to this time . . . come back indoors, why don't you rest . . . you must rest from all your praying sometime, lay down the holy book, won't you. You've been sitting all night over your reading again . . . uttering cries . . . worshipping . . . paying no attention to mortal voices [*she has appeared in the door*]. Petrus . . . awake from your wrestling with God . . . look upon His world . . . the new dawn calls the coalminers to go down under the earth again . . . and today does not find you a rested workman . . . the golden morn is at the door . . . my God—the golden morn is at the door . . . [*she looks up to the sky*] it is calling you too to go underground. [*off into the house*].

PETRUS HEISSLER: *lost in thought, speaks*] The golden morn is at the door . . . yes . . . and over there . . . are you not laughing, that war dwells in all the streets . . . and over there the murderer lies . . . sprawled over the table . . . sleeping softly like a dead man after a victory feast . . . slay not one locust . . . for the whole swarm cometh . . . you must proclaim the GREAT WAR. [*Off into the house*].

FOUR TINY VILLAGE BOYS: *come marching along with German flags, singing*]

Sie sollen ihn nicht haben,
den freien, deutschen Rhein,
wenn sie wie gierige Raben,
sich heiser danach schrei'n . . . [*Off*]

PETRUS HEISSLER: *appears again, quite poorly clad like a beggar, exactly as he has been sitting all night over the Bible, bare-footed and with*

42

unkempt, shaggy grey hair, a straw bundle and a scarlet rag tied to a pole, marches out of the house, solemnly past the palace park, calling out now all the time] Flames will writhe from the eaves of the houses like scarlet banners . . . starving children will wriggle between rotting corpses like maggots . . . no help will come . . . women will gasp their last under the lust of blood-drunk men . . . no help will come . . . all screams will shriek hopelessly into the air . . . all groans, such as the tortured groan, will reach hopelessly into the air . . . this will be THE GREAT WAR. *[Off]*

A group of well-dressed RENTIERS *come along the street from behind the village.* SCHALAST, *Secretary to the* MINISTER, *is speaking to them. So that the* RENTIERS *crowd round to hear what he has to say.*

SCHALAST: Of course, the rumour is going the rounds of every newspaper . . . every street . . . every office . . . being blabbered in all the coffee shops in the cities, is the subject of bragging and boasting in streets and squares . . . bragging and boasting in all the stock-exchanges . . . and because the government naturally has to be careful with gold for military purposes . . . it has only itself to blame in a sense . . . for His Excellency has naturally instructed the Post Office and indeed all official Banking Agencies to hold on to gold and to pay out only in paper money.

APTEKA: *rentier, a small bent man]* Of course . . . that will be the case . . . if it can't be otherwise . . . I've just been to early mass . . . I even thought I detected a whisper of the rumour in the Priest's words . . . yes, yes, yes . . . My dear Ministerial Secretary . . . Mr. Schalast . . . what we'd really like to know is what the outlook is for the Stock Market . . . just tell us, Mr. Schalast . . . War . . . I beg you . . . what does His Excellency say to this terrible war-mongering . . . I should have thought that in our culture and civilisation we'd be beyond that . . .

OTREMBA: *slyly]* One can quite simply and clearly weigh up and calculate the arguments for and against . . . war would be the most senseless waste of money . . . not just barbarism . . . the most criminal waste of money.

APTEKA: *quickly*] My dear Mr. Schalast . . . even a child can grasp the fact that if our national income is to increase, then it depends on a slow and steady development of the great concerns of our civilization . . . I beg you . . . what's to become of our colossal factories if the work-people on both sides and in all corners of the world are making corpses and cripples of themselves on battlefields . . . what's to become of our machines . . . or our great inventions, if there is no work-force there to make them work . . . and it depends above all on the stability of the channels supplying finance . . . above all the banks must be able to work in peace, for if the financial life of the nation were to grind to a halt . . .

SCHALAST: Gently, gently . . . they're all still fast asleep in the palace . . . won't you come round the back with me to the offices . . . [*They have stopped at the gates*]. You are quite right Mr. Apteka . . . it's this way. His Excellency is sure to be still asleep . . . only Her Highness, the Princess, who suffers permanently from insomnia, will be awake already . . . and to the annoyance of His Excellency is sure to be croaking her Jeremiad of war too, nothing but war . . . you know, croaking her Jeremiad, that really is taking malicious pleasure in talking of the devil and wondering if he'll appear . . . for the gentle lady loves to do just that . . . Prophesying from dreams that she has already seen, let's say, red and white army hordes here on our fields and meadows riding against each other in the blood-bath of wild battle . . .

MINISTER KAIL *has stepped out of one of the palace doors. In very respectful posture and with a deep bow which is not answered,* SCHALAST *goes with the rentiers round the side of the palace and they disappear.* MINISTER KAIL *goes up to one of the terrace tables, which* CASPAR *the servant has silently laid already. A lackey is just bringing the paper. At this moment* ENOCH KAIL *in Hussar's uniform and spurs but with head bare appears at the French window cautiously, takes a tentative step forward.*

CASPAR: Our young master, the Count is waiting respectfully . . .
MINISTER KAIL: Who . . . the young Count . . . yes . . . what is one to do . . . if one has but one heir to carry on one's

name . . . and he gets up to all sorts of despicable tricks on the sly . . . and wallows around with doubtful females from the scum of the people . . . tell the young Count . . . tell him nothing . . . let him stand and wait . . . till he too gets angry for once . . . till at last the ache in his blood tells him that his father despises him . . . just let him stand there . . . tell him, the Prince cannot recall that he has anything else to discuss with the young Count, which was not already abundantly clear . . . tell him . . . the Prince has duties, which make his time too precious to waste on his son's shabby tricks . . .

ENOCH KAIL *looks at the* PRINCE *with an embarrassed smile. Starts to say something, suppresses it.*

MINISTER KAIL: *now very quietly*] I have nothing more to say to a forger—now or ever.

ENOCH KAIL *withdraws undecidedly to the door without daring to say a word, with the same embarrassed smile on his face. Off.*

MINISTER KAIL: Outside these four walls no-one must ever dare to utter the slightest word about this Caspar . . . is that clear?

CASPAR: As you command, Your Excellency . . . [*Off*].

ANOTHER SERVANT: *appears*] Your Private Secretary, Excellency.

MINISTER KAIL *beckons,* SCHALAST *enters with the mail.*

MINISTER KAIL: *sitting at the breakfast table, opens a letter. Suddenly animated*] All this rebellious talk of war will upset even the most rational of men in the long run . . .

SCHALAST: If Your Excellency will permit me . . . in the smaller towns some of the banks were really stormed yesterday.

MINISTER KAIL: For heaven's sake, don't . . . war in this day and age . . . why, nowadays we can estimate simply and clearly the arguments for and against . . . War would be the most senseless waste of money . . . not merely the most dreadful barbarism . . . the most criminal waste of money . . . now you listen, Schalast, . . . the leading ministers of the civilised nations are fully aware of their enormous responsibility . . . war in this day and age would be a true blasphemy against the welfare of every modern industrial nation . . . the people themselves know that now . . . and as long as I am at the helm . . . my dear Schalast . . . see that this is made immediately and explicitly clear to all who want to hear it on my authority . . .

SCHALAST: It shall be as you command, Your Excellency . . . [*Off*].

MINISTER KAIL: *eating breakfast and reading letters; meanwhile the servant* CASPAR *has re-appeared* [*Pause*]] Caspar . . . enquire . . . whether Her Highness is awake yet.

MATER MARIA SALESIA: *steps timidly out onto the terrace*] Her Highness enjoyed a miraculously refreshing sleep last night . . . Her Highness even claims, such as only in her childhood . . . and Her Highness is filled with an almost childlike gaiety . . .

MINISTER KAIL: *leaps up agitatedly*] Yes, I'm sure . . . as soon as these incomprehensible characters hear of war, plague, starvation, they begin to be happy . . . I know how it goes . . . that one must love suffering . . . that one must despise the goods of this world. The rats and mice always want to gnaw a hole in honour, and power, and wealth [*rages up and down*] against honour, power and wealth the religious types have always been ready to regurgitate the sacrilegious slogans of the agitators . . .

MATER MARIA SALESIA: I thank you, Your Excellency . . . for this compliment . . .

MINISTER KAIL: *still agitated, raging up and down*] Rubbish . . . don't bring up all that business of yours about the crosses and crowns of this world . . . you and your higher life . . . I'd just like to clap eyes on these spoiled creatures when they no longer know in which silken bed they will sleep and in which marble vault their noble bones will rest in the princely park . . . and I say that in contempt of myself too.

MATER MARIA SALESIA: *withdrawing backwards into the house*] I too fail to grasp the cruel conviction of this strange woman . . . we devout sisters pray to a gentle saviour . . . who is a God of Peace . . . who teaches us to love even our enemies . . . [*off*]

PRINCESS KAIL: *looks out of an upstairs window*] Oh, no . . . he said explicitly . . . 'I am come, not to bring Peace, but the Sword'. [*Off immediately*].

MINISTER KAIL *is transfixed staring at the window. Three* ARCH-ANGELS *with scrolls in their hands stride out of the village and disappear into the houses and the palace, taking notice of no-one.*

PETRUS HEISSLER: *still not visible, calling in the distance*] God is crueller than the forces of animality . . . boundless as the immeasurable sky . . . be not afraid of the infinite . . . God is the great fire-raiser . . . God is the ultimate mystery . . . God will measure out eternity . . . God will go even further . . . this will be the Great War . . .

Miners and other working people, with bundles in their hands, assemble on the village street, forming up.

PETRUS HEISSLER: *strides among them*] God is a hand which reaches out to you from on high . . . blessed be he who sees the hand . . .

Out of the palace stream women, dressed as nurses, who hurry away.

MINISTER KAIL: *stirring from his stupor*] Caspar . . . what's going on here . . . Caspar . . .

PETRUS HEISSLER: *interrupting with cries*] But God's body is also a cloud of scurrying, grey mist . . . the awful screaming emptiness . . . a myriad vortex of men slaying each other . . . be watchful . . . be men . . . be manly and be strong . . . this will be the Great War.

A column of conscripts, some wearing army caps, all with bundles in their hand, march past singing:

Ich kenn' ein'n hellen Edelstein von köstlich hoher Art,
in einem stillen Kämmerlein, da liegt er gut verwahrt.
Kein Demant ist, der diesem gleicht, so weit der liebe Himmel
    reicht—
Die Menschenbrust ists Kämmerlein,
da legte Gott so tief hinein,
den schönen, hellen Edelstein,
das treue, deutsche Herz . . .

(A priceless treasure I know well, of rare and cunning art;
In a secret chamber doth it dwell, I would not with it part.
No diamond can with it compare; no star that shines is half
    so fair.

47

The human bosom is its throne
'Twas hidden there by God alone
This beauteous, brilliant precious stone
A true and German heart.)

The group of men assembled in the village joins on and takes up the song.

PETRUS HEISSLER: *screams as loud as he can*] Force against Force . . . murderers against murderers . . . murderous nations against murderous nations . . . this will be the Great War . . .

The PRINCESS *herself, dressed as a nurse and accompanied by the* MATER, *hurries out of the palace after the main stream.*

PETRUS HEISSLER: *as he disappears*] This will be the Great War . . .
PRINCESS KAIL: *suddenly looks back, hurries over to* MINISTER KAIL *and says with quivering voice*] Oh, you . . . Prince and Master . . . mankind cannot be tamed . . . and now there will be the Great War . . . Once again primitive passions will know no bounds . . . and even you will be just an individual human being again . . . capable of deeds and crimes . . . capable of everything . . . and even you will be only a poor sacrifice . . . for now the time of human sacrifice will begin again . . . farewell . . . beloved man . . . father of Enoch . . .

They both, PRINCESS *and* MATER, *hurry after the column.*

MINISTER KAIL: *who up till now has let everything go past him as if he were petrified*] Caspar . . . have I gone mad . . . am I not Prime Minister any more . . . am I no longer the Prince . . . the world is moving of its own volition . . . what's happening then . . . there's going to be a war . . . No, No, there's not going to be a war . . . the car . . . quick . . . the car . . . to the king . . . is the king still king . . . Caspar . . . is the king still king . . . [*Off into the palace*].

ENOCH KAIL *as Hussar officer, in battle order, a riding-crop under his arm, appears in the park.*

GRUSCHKA: *comes hurrying from the village. Everything she now says to him is intermingled with tears and laughter*] The Archangels . . . the angels of war . . . shall trumpet splendid music about you . . . [*They stride on.* GRUSCHKA *clings to* ENOCH'S *arm. She strokes him repeatedly, weeping and laughing*] Think of me, Enoch . . . if you should have to breathe your last . . . you . . . Enoch . . . yet it is you I am carrying living in my womb . . . kiss me once again . . . yet it is you I am carrying living in my womb . . . and though you lay as one dead on the ground hewn down on the field of battle, yet out of my womb shall I bear you living once more—oh, Enoch.

ENOCH KAIL: You know, Gruschka . . . I am not even aware that I am saying goodbye to all my past life . . . to father and mother and family home . . . to everything . . . I am so deeply moved . . . I wanted to confess my past before my father once again . . . but the past fades away like an empty echo . . . now I can no longer look back . . . forget . . . criminal . . . spendthrift and gambler . . . he who grasps the sword and then looks behind him, is not called to the kingdom of God . . . now the time of human sacrifices will begin . . . now I am aflame, to gamble my own life . . . don't cry, Gruschka . . . darling . . . you must laugh and be gay . . . for in your swelling womb I am safe . . . [*petting her like a child*] and you will carry me and tend me . . . a new, little Enoch . . . one who is rejuvenated . . . one who is washed quite pure . . . in the hot blood of the beloved . . .

GRUSCHKA: *embracing him and not letting him go*] Enoch, I am your wife and your mother . . . I must stay behind . . . a pregnant woman cannot cast stones against the enemy . . . I must stay behind . . . to tend you in my womb . . . believe me, Enoch. [*He has freed himself and marched on a little*] I shall walk with you just a little further . . . till you mount your horse . . . now that the Great War gleams . . . and the high Archangels swing their scythes and reap the harvest . . . oh, Enoch . . . who can hold the other back.

They have disappeared after the column. Now from the village a long column of disciplined infantry marches past singing:

Es braust ein Ruf, wie Donnerhall,
wie Schwertgeklirr und Wogenprall . . .
zum Rhein, zum Rhein, zum deutschen Rhein . . .
Wer will des Stromes Hüter sein? . . .
Lieb Vaterland, magst ruhig sein,
fest steht und treu die Wacht am Rhein! . . .

The call goes up, the hills rebound,
With clashing steel the waves do sound . . .
The Rhine, the Rhine, to the German Rhine . . .
Who can defend this noble line?
Dear fatherland, peace now be thine,
Strong hearts and true, we'll watch our Rhine! . . .

While the song can still be heard and the stream of people ebbs, THREE HORRIFIC FIGURES *appear singly one after the other. Rat-faces with prominent, ugly incisors, their clothing perfidiously fantastic, stilettoes at their side. The figures bent and spiteful, squinting, from screwed-up eyes. Watchful and listening. Little crowns of bones in their hair. They have belts and adornments made out of rope-ends from hangings, and all sorts of animal skulls and human bones. They peer furtively into all windows in the village.*

FIRST: Empty . . . [*passes on*] An old wife in bed . . .
SECOND: A child in the cradle . . . [*passes on*] A fat woman in
bed, face all bandaged up, an old woman sitting by the fire . . .
THIRD: A ninety-year-old man . . . no teeth at all . . . muttering
prayers to himself for a peaceful end . . . everybody who can
walk . . . women and children have gone off with the men
. . . hihihihi . . . even the princely palace looks empty . . .

As they approach it the PORTER *appears on the terrace and comes towards them at the gates, the great bunch of keys in his hand.*

PORTER: Holy Jesus . . . the Great War is declared . . . so many
trumpets sound from Lord knows where all, that one's ears are
buzzing all the time . . . women and children are running like
crazy to the great blood-letting . . . what on earth do you
want here?

FIRST: *grinning scornfully*] Nothing for the time being.

PORTER: Who are you anyway . . .

FIRST: *grinning spitefully*] Servants . . . helpful spirits . . . ambassadors of a higher power . . . war is our master . . . war is our employer . . .

SECOND: *grinning spitefully*] Once the BIG BLOOD BATH really starts, we help the slaughter along, on the sly . . . hihihi . . . we spit poison into the blood of the wounded . . . and into the blood of women and children too—poison . . . that the earth may be free again from the plague of mankind . . . hihihi . . .

THIRD: *grinning spitefully*] We bring dysentery—cholera—the plague —fever in all temperatures . . . hot as hell . . . with hallucinations to make your hair stand on end . . . what you will . . . madness to scorch your bones dry . . . hihihi . . .

The PORTER, *seized with horror, slinks back into the palace.*

THE THREE HORRIFIC FIGURES: *hobbling away pitifully on crutches*] Not feeling hungry, Mr. Porter? . . . the menu was enough . . . hihihi . . . Not feeling hungry, Mr. Porter? . . . the menu was enough . . . hihihi . . . And such a pretty bill of fare.

As they laugh spitefully darkness descends over the scene.

PART THREE

*As the darkness disperses the workers' houses are seen to be on a wartime
footing. So too the palace. Two* NAPOLEONIC GRENADIERS *stand guard
at the foot of the steps. French Guard posts are quartered in one of the
village houses. Gun pyramids outside it. Single soldiers stand about
outside the door. On a tree trunk lying crosswise outside the door other
soldiers are sitting playing cards. Corpses lie around here and there.
Wine is being served by a* CANTEEN WOMAN *from an open wine cask.
Now and then cannons can be heard thundering in the distance.*

THE CANTEEN WOMAN: Yes, yes . . . thunder away . . . rumble
on . . . we know . . . you're using human skulls for targets . . .

ONE OF THE DRINKING SOLDIERS: Battle is battle . . . War is war
. . . you can't expect soldiers to throw confetti at each other
. . . stupid whore . . .

Other soldiers laugh.

CANTEEN WOMAN: At long last they had him forged fast to the
lonely rock in the ocean . . . WAR . . . may he be cursed
. . . the Great War . . . at long last they had forged him with
chains to the rock . . . as is right and proper for such a superhuman fellow . . .

ONE OF THE SOLDIERS: What are you babbling about anyway . . .
who are you spewing your bile at . . .

CANTEEN WOMAN: At the great criminal . . . the great murderer
. . . at long last they had him forged fast to the lonely rock in
the ocean . . . because he whirls up nations and kings into
wild confusion . . . and if he could he would pile up a world
state out of human bodies . . . the whole earth burns beneath
his tread . . .

A GAMBLING SOLDIER: Hahahaha . . . let the old earth burn . . .
better stars than this have burned out already . . .

ANOTHER SOLDIER: Mind you don't pull your bad tempered mug
out of shape . . . you lovely lady of the canteen wagon, you

nagging sausage virgin . . . raped three times by Satan himself
. . . and plucked and fingered by a hundred bloody hands . . .
the battlefield is no nursery . . . there it's a case of life or
death . . .

CANTEEN WOMAN: *has thrown a tin mug at him*] Wretches . . .
beasts . . . blood-thirsty murderous villains . . . that's what
you are, all of you . . .

SECOND GAMBLER: Ten of diamonds . . . ace of diamonds . . .

CANTEEN WOMAN: *mad with rage*] Bearded beast-face . . . spurred
and booted wildcat . . . you won't talk me into revelling in
massacre.

SECOND GAMBLER: Ace of clubs . . . king of clubs . . . trump
. . . why don't you shut your hairy trap . . . boozy bitch . . .

ANOTHER SOLDIER: I'll batter your bulging chest in with a rifle
butt . . . big-bosomed bitch . . . like I did that young
lieutenant of Hussars yesterday . . . he choked to death in his
own blood straight off . . . [*rumble of cannons can be heard again*].

CANTEEN WOMAN: *shaking her clenched fist in the direction of the
cannon-bursts*] Yes, yes . . . thunder away . . . just rumble on
. . . we know . . . the executioner is behind us already with
his axe at our throats . . . you would strangle me in cold
animal lust, if you could, like any enemy woman . . . blasted
werwolf . . .

FIRST GAMBLER: Take . . . that . . . and that . . . earthlouse.

SECOND GAMBLER: Wha-a-t [*he has grabbed him by the wrist*] You
dog . . . dirty jackal . . . you are even ready to cheat with
Death's claw clenched tight round your throat . . . and the
blasted Death's Head grinning at us all already.

FIRST GAMBLER: *pushes him away and reaches for the cards*] Gold . . .
gold . . . that's all I need . . . as long as I'm alive . . .

CANTEEN WOMAN: Hahahaha . . . gold is all I need . . . for gold
you can buy heaven and earth . . . and God and the devil into
the bargain . . . gold is always what counts . . . gold is the
key to the kingdom for heaven on earth . . . yes, that's true
enough . . .

SECOND GAMBLER: *grabs the first gambler by the arm and then by the
throat. Other soldiers come closer*] Gold is the key to the kingdom
of heaven . . . cheating swine . . . [*They tussle*].

A THIRD SOLDIER: Bash his skull in . . . beat his brains in . . .

[*the first gambler is beaten down with much noise and laughter from the others . . . Roar of cannons*]

NINETY- YEAR-OLD MAN: *hobbles out of village hut next door*] Quiet, quiet please, dear people . . .

FIRST HORRIFIC FIGURE: *pokes head out of door, behind him grinning*] Hihihihi . . . you just wait, my hearty . . . just wait . . . you harum-scarum . . . you'd just love to leap on the meadow, my little foal . . . hihihihi . . . you'd like to be taking part in real LIFE . . . you little fool, you . . . you imagine probably now that you are ninety you've learned once for all how to dance and hop to the music in the hurly-burly of war . . . [*suddenly stretches up to his full height and spreads out his hand so that one can see he has vulture's claws*] Lie down with the dead, my son . . . no more hurly-burly . . . no more horror music . . . [*he has seized the ninety-year-old by the neck. Ninety-year-old collapses*].

A RAGGED WOMAN: *near the door*] There . . . no mouth is ever shut at the moment of death . . . the breath's expelled . . . when the soul has departed with the last sigh, the jaws gape wide . . . the dead always look as if they're to yawn through all eternity . . . [*Other ragged women have wondered over from the village*]

A RAGGED WOMAN: *with a child, has wandered in through the gates, right up to the* GRENADIERS *standing guard*] Oh, Sir . . .

FIRST GRENADIER: What do you want?

THE CHILD: *cries while the mother searches one of the bodies*] To waken the dead.

FIRST GRENADIER: You can't waken the dead.

RAGGED WOMAN: *wailing*] To bury the dead.

SECOND GRENADIER: You can't bury the dead just now . . . you idiots . . . the battle is still raging . . . has been for days . . . and piles dead upon dead . . .

PORTER: *comes round the palace*] Clear off to the fields . . . and rip up roots if you're hungry . . . this is the master's park and the Prince's palace must be guarded . . . an important personage is living here now . . .

CANTEEN WOMAN: *tapping a fresh cask*] Fresh brandy, folks . . . drink your fill . . . till the blind rage surges into the blood . . . if you have to go into the murderous tumult, then you won't see the horrors when harried men slaughter each other . . .

MANY SOLDIERS: *have grabbed tin mugs and started drinking toasts*] Long Live the Great War . . . Long Live the Great War . . .

Out of PETRUS HEISSLER'S *window peers one of the* HORRIFIC FIGURES. *Some of the rabble recoil from the grin.*

THE HORRIFIC FIGURE: Hihihihi . . . no need to be afraid . . . you old bag of bones . . . the war won't eat you . . . hihihihi . . . come on . . . I just want to show you something really funny . . . just come up to the window here . . . there . . . he . . . sits.

THE WOMAN: *staring into the window*] Huh . . . why, it's a couple . . .

THE HORRIFIC FIGURE: Hihihi . . . but of course it's a couple . . . a rotting female corpse . . . and the War Prophet himself who is so scared he'd crawl into a mouse-hole if he could only find one . . . for the time being he has just crawled behind his bed . . . to escape the tumult of war.

THE STARING WOMEN: *call*] Petrus Heissler . . . Petrus Heissler.

From the window an unarticulated, idiotic scream can be heard.

THE HORRIFIC FIGURE: Hihihihi . . . a rotting female corpse . . . and a manly man, already mad with fear . . . listen won't you . . . the prophet of doom is bleating like a calf . . . now he is afraid of the living . . . hihihihi . . . he prefers to hold onto the rotting corpse of his wife—since murder is the watch-word in the world . . . hihihihi.

TERRIFIED WOMAN: Look, servants are scattering flowers and laurel wreaths on the flag-stones . . .

PORTER: Quiet there . . . be off with you . . . clear off to the fields . . . this is the Great Lord's park . . .

A FRENCH GENERAL: *comes hurriedly from the village to the palace*] Where is Our Great Leader?

SECOND GENERAL: *immediately after him*] More reserves must go up the line, the enemies' centre must be broken . . . [*They hurry up the terrace and try to enter the palace*]

A VALET: *has appeared in the door—worriedly*] Our Great Leader dreams alone in the Great Hall.

THE GENERALS: *undecided and laughing*] Eh . . . what's that . . . sacred cannon balls . . . madness . . . Our Great Leader dreams alone in the Great Hall . . .

VALET: *mysteriously*] He is dreaming like a seraph . . .
GENERALS: He is dreaming like a seraph . . .

Round the palace surge French soldiers in rout, with whom the two Generals rush off in agitation.

LEADING OFFICER: Forwards . . . not into these houses . . . advance . . . advance . . .
THE OFFICER OF A SECOND CLOSED COLUMN OF RUSSIANS: Not into these houses . . . on . . . on . . . we must reach cover . . . a hundred yards on . . . at the double . . . march, march.
CANTEEN WOMAN: Yes, yes . . . thunder on . . . roar on . . . till the earth trembles . . . we know . . . the executioner is standing waiting behind us already with his axe . . .

Wounded German soldiers, Russians too, Italians, Austrians, Scandinavians, etc., are carried on by ambulance men. A young German Hussar officer in a faint. As the nurse bends over him, he wakes . . . he is

ENOCH KAIL: Sister . . . come close . . . sister . . . quick . . . quick . . . pluck me some green clover . . . pluck me red clover . . . a bundle of gold clover . . . quick, quick . . . for death comes . . . lay a bunch of clover blossoms over my twisted mouth . . . death comes . . . yes . . . death comes . . . in the grim service of murder . . . death comes . . . [*babbling and breathing his last*]
CANTEEN WOMAN: *sings meanwhile*]

As I was walking all alane
I heard twa corbies making a mane:
The tane unto the tither did say,
'Whar shall we gang and dine the day?'
'—In behint yon auld fail dyke
I wot there lies a new-slain knight;
And naebody kens that he lies there
But his hawk, his hound, and his lady fair.
'Ye'll sit on his white house-bane,
And I'll pike out his bonny blue e'en:
Wi' ae lock o' his gowden hair
We'll theek our nest when it grows bare.'

Meanwhile a small column of bearers has marched up, carrying gigantic sides of meat on poles.

CANTEEN WOMAN: Quick, lay on a row of open fires . . . the combat soldiers must be stuffed afresh . . . they must get new strength . . . because the death-healing will go on and on . . .

ONE OF THE BEARERS: A fire . . . quick . . .

CANTEEN WOMAN: Yes, yes . . . don't stop to think . . . hang the whole sides of meat on iron bars over the bright flames . . . at least till the fat starts to crackle . . . so that your harassed, starved comrades don't have to gulp their meat still bloody

. . . [*Various scattered soldiers rush past*]

CANTEEN WOMAN: Stuff yourselves with cattle carcasses . . . till blind madness rages in the blood . . . and you can murder on . . . [*The soldiers circle the fire greedily and cut themselves chunks of meat from the sides and continue their assault*] At long last they had forged him to the lonely island in the ocean . . . War . . . a curse on him, the great war . . . at long last they had forged him with chains to the rock . . . as is right and proper with such a superhuman fellow . . . but now the master criminal has burst his chains once again . . . and is among us . . . every living being now carries live ammunition, fifty bullets in his belt . . . and 200 bullets in his pack . . . every single bullet aimed at the heart of his neighbour . . .

A FRENCH GENERAL: *comes on once again*] Where is the Great Leader . . .

ANOTHER GENERAL: *immediately after him*] Our attack on the villages and the centre has been repulsed by the enemy yet again . . .

WOMEN: *crowding round*] They are laying a laurel-wreath on a golden table.

VALET: *appearing in the palace door*] Our relentless leader will appear this very moment . . . Porter [*pushing back the women*] Away there . . . we must have absolute quiet . . . the relentless Lord of War himself lives here . . .

WOMEN: *cringing back*] The relentless Lord . . . huh . . . the Lord of War . . .

All the people and soldiers have suddenly become alert, looking expectantly towards the palace portal.

SOME SOLDIERS: *also shout*] The War Lord . . . attention . . . the Lord of War.

Out of the ruined palace door with trumpet blasts of the Archangels stirring and fading again in the ether for a moment, steps the ESCAPED VISIONARY, *a withered little man with a Napoleonic face, who is enveloped in vast grey rags. Barefoot, iron rings on his wrists and ankles . . . short ends of chain on them. Quite lost in thought.*

PEOPLE AND SOLDIERS: *cheer* Hurrah . . . hurrah . . . hurrah . . .
PETRUS HEISSLER: *completely ragged, half naked state, baaing and bleating, suddenly comes rushing out of his house door, runs at the terrified women, who flee from him, stops, trumpets with his voice into his hands as into a horn. And then sinks down on his knees with face uplifted and shouts out his prayer*] Our Father, which art in Heaven, hallowed be Thy name, Thy Kingdom come, Thy will be done on earth, as it is in heaven.

A shiver of terror passes through the frightened women, all cringe away.

THE FRIGHTENED WOMAN: Huuuuh . . .
PETRUS HEISSLER *is struck dead by a bullet.*
PEOPLE AND SOLDIERS: *without taking any notice shout*] Hurrah . . . hurrah . . . hurrah . . .
THE ESCAPED VISIONARY: *hard and proud and timid, looking into the crowd, and occasionally shivering as with cold and wrapping his rag coat closer round him, talking to himself*] They forged me fast with chains of brass to the lonely rock in the ocean . . . so that my wrists and my ankles bled . . .
SOME TIMID VOICES: Huh . . . he looks as if he came from the tomb.
ESCAPED VISIONARY: They call me the Master Criminal . . . they call me the great murderer . . . because I dream like a seraph . . . because my will flies like the sure arrow of a God into the furthest light . . . because no barrier of space or of time ever

fenced in my will . . . who could bury me for dead in a stony grave . . . I shall live, be it in rusting chains of men . . . or bold and free . . . I shall live as long as human bodies live . . . and the earth breathes . . .

OTHER VOICES: He looks as if he came from eternity . . .

OTHER VOICES: He looks as if he had broken free from chains and bonds . . .

OTHER VOICES: Who has released him . . .

OTHER VOICES: Perhaps Archangels have burst his chains . . .

ESCAPED VISIONARY: You recoil from me, you peoples of the earth . . . and yet I bring you the salvation of this earth . . .

The wounded try to raise themselves up . . . soldiers and people all crowd closer. The gamblers have stopped gambling.

ALL VOICES: *shout anew*] Hurrah . . . hurrah . . . hurrah . . .

Through the hurrahs can be heard louder and louder:

TERRIFIED VOICES: Bread . . . bread . . . oh, sir . . . the corn of our fields is trampled down . . . we are doomed to starvation . . . [*Interspersed with*]

OTHER CRIES: We are being slain . . . brother by brother . . . oh, sire . . . help . . . help . . . help . . .

ESCAPED VISIONARY: I am the force against force . . . I am the destruction against destruction . . . I am the merciless heart against the merciless heart . . . I hunt in the clouds . . . my coat of rags flies in the storm wind . . . my word is command . . . at my word a hundred fall dead and bleeding on the brown earth . . . my gesture is command . . . at my gesture a thousand fiery lancers storm like a cloud of death over the fields and kill . . . my glance is command . . . at my glance ten thousand murderous bullets scream through the air and kill . . . like swarms of birds of prey . . .

A GROUP OF NURSES: *attempt to force a way through*] We have no more room for the dying.

OTHER NURSES: There are so many wounded and mutilated we can no longer bandage them.

OTHER SISTERS: *shout*] They are being mown down in swathes.

THE VISIONARY *grows bolder and bolder the more they moan.*

PRINCESS KAIL: *as nurse calls*]. We need first-aid stations . . . stretchers . . . beds . . . soft beds . . . mattresses . . . pillows . . . blankets . . . the dying are legion . . . heroes — every one . . .

A SISTER: *calls*] O Jesus and Mary . . . have pity . . . we can't talk to the dying of the Kingdom of Heaven any more.

ESCAPED VISIONARY: *again as if to himself*] My kingdom is of this world only [*straightening up*] I surge along dark as a thunderstorm . . . burning as bright and light as a fiery breath that sets village and city aflame . . . I am the great assassin . . . I have the winged boldness to carry me over all the misery of the earth . . . despite coat of rags . . . an armoured cherub . . . [*he reaches for the laurel on the table*] the wreath is mine . . . [*he presses the laurel wreath on to his bald skull*]. The crown is mine . . . *While from their litters with fixed, radiant eyes, even the wounded drag themselves forward to the* ESCAPED VISIONARY, *a rousing cheer bursts forth:* Oh, sire . . . oh, radiant sire.

ESCAPED VISIONARY: *with regal gesture immediately silences the shouts, so that again there is deathly silence and only a few cannon bursts roar, punctuate his words . . . with increasing lack of restraint, more and more ecstatic*] My horizon is as wide as the bounds of the earth . . . I feel a promise boiling in my breast . . . I hear final choruses shatter the air, like victory celebrations . . . I hear the rejoicing of the morning stars . . . there . . . there . . . far . . . far . . .

Among the people an exultant war song stirs, arms start to swing, feet to march. Silenced again by a gesture from the ESCAPED VISIONARY:

I see it shining in the dawn light . . . realms of mankind [*Exultant tumult around him*]; sunny, blissful realms of mankind . . . man with man in peace side by side, like the silent twinkling stars . . . [*Exultant tumult all around him*].

CONFUSED VOICES: *calling*] We built you a triumphal carriage of gold . . . radiant superman. [*With much cheering a coach of gold is brought on*].

ESCAPED VISIONARY: Ah . . . ah . . . you slave spirits . . . you grey moths . . . you miserable scum . . . I am the Great War . . .

The golden carriage has been driven forward, so that the ESCAPED
VISIONARY *can leap quickly on to it, while now all the people,
including the bleeding and wounded soldiers, women, children, nurses,
put themselves in harness in front of it; turn the wheels or push it
from behind.*

ESCAPED VISIONARY: *has seized the golden whip sticking up on the
coach and makes it whistle through the air*] Roll, golden coach,
through streams of human blood . . . [*He whips the people
harnessed in front*] Crushing millions . . . ah . . . ah . . . I
will drive into the new dawn . . . I will give you all the
kingdoms of the earth and all the glory thereof . . . there . . .
far . . . far . . . in the morning light . . . in the morning
light . . .

Amidst thunderous choruses of ARCHANGELS *and the violent whip-
lashes of the* ESCAPED VISIONARY *the cheering crowd has dragged the
coach forward, till it disappears from sight. The cheering and* ARCH-
ANGEL *choruses can be heard echoing back for some time, while
suddenly the empty stage blacks out. Then as the choruses of the*
ARCHANGELS *swell anew a dull chorus of the dead from human
throats begins to mingle with it, which becomes more and more
predominant. And lit by pale twilight there appears from the side
where the golden coach with the* ESCAPED VISIONARY *had disappeared
a solemn army column, all Death's Heads in tattered uniforms
marching endlessly across to the opposite side with funeral music
swelling more and more horribly. Thereupon the deepest darkness
settles over the scene.*

PART FOUR

*Out of the darkness in the light of the stars appears the same place as in
the first three parts. Barriers and fences are all destroyed. Only a portion
of the palace wall with the front portal and the terrace with a smashed
marble figure is still standing. Also a small remnant of iron railing.
Trees and bushes have nearly all disappeared . . . A few bushes have
survived by the broken railing. Paths and streets are overgrown. The
village is now overgrown ruins, with some bolt-holes like earth mounds.
At the furthest end of the plain one can see an engrossed, gentle old man,
FATHER FRANCIS, building a little temple. In silent engrossed labour he
carries up tree trunks and beams so that in the course of the scene a small
wooden temple grows up out of the ground. It is very early tentative
spring. A hairy* CRIPPLE *with only his right arm peeps fearfully out of
his bolt-hole. He looks all about him and slowly takes a few steps,
carefully sniffing the air. He is quite covered in grey hair, wears a short
ragged smock*): It is still night . . . the earth seems empty still
. . . everybody still cowering in their rat-holes . . . look . . .
a stag standing in the field . . . [*he pulls a rope out of his pocket
and lifts a stone, and quickly ties the rope onto it*] wait a minute . . .
I'll take my sling and kill the horned monarch [*He throws and
races off suddenly like a sprinter*].

ANOTHER CRIPPLE: *he too quite ravaged and hairy, also looks out
fearfully from his bit of ruin*] Was it really one eternal, dark,
dreadful night . . . or was it only the deep dark of human
sleep, I should like to know . . . [*he takes a few steps and looks
thoughtfully at the hole in the ground*]. In any event that is a hole
in the ground . . . and there is deep silence in the air . . .
and if I didn't know that it is a truly wonderful silence, I should
think it the sweetest of music . . . and that the breezes are
soft hands . . . women's hands . . . [*he looks at the sky*] yes
. . . where am I anyway . . . true . . . the stars too are still
there . . . or have they too lost their splendour with the
great killing . . . and quite lost their course . . . no . . .
there they are up there . . . and still shining . . . I recognise

them all . . . there is the fixed point . . . the Pole Star . . . [*He turns round and points to the East*] and there, that is the point where the sun always used to rise over the night . . . so that it became wonderful and warm . . . and everything became quite golden . . . [*he intones*] 'The day cometh forth as a bridegroom out of his chamber and rejoiceth as a giant to run his course' and if I am not mistaken . . . perhaps a new dawn is breaking . . . the War must be over . . .

A THIRD CRIPPLE: *also rather ravaged-looking, climbs out of his bolt-hole and looks around fearfully. When he sees the other cripple outside his hole he crawls back in fear*] There is another . . . human being, who has also awakened . . . hahahaha . . . another miserable cripple . . . one with a stump of an arm . . . and hacked-off fingers . . . the eye-teeth shot away . . . he keeps pressing his side as if he still had a bullet in the hip bone . . . his head is the only bit not in ruins . . . Yes . . . if my head, for instance, had been smashed in the great Witches' Sabbath, I would now be lying here beneath the daisies . . . [*More solitary, timid cripples, all with sticks in their hands or dragging their feet, wander in the dawn over the field*] . . . and these greedy cripples could dig me out with their sticks too—and would possibly find a stinking carrion of a man right under the top layer of earth . . . [*When the other cripple just stares fearfully and sharply at him*]. No, I don't dare go out . . . I don't trust things yet . . . [*He has disappeared into his bolt-hole again*].

ONE OF THE CRIPPLES: *who are examining and probing the ground with a stick*] Under the surface lie the most marvellous treasures from the old days . . . not just bomb splinters, ladies' jewellery too . . . fine glasses . . . look at this, for instance, a silver beaker . . . I've even dug out a silver beaker with my stick . . . [*he has held up the silver beaker, looks around him fearfully and puts it away*]. Is the war still on . . . I've tried everything to find out . . . well . . . at least the hellish noise has gone . . . the fearful murderous screams have gone . . . that showered from all sides like pitch black storms . . . cast me down unconscious . . . and left me behind, a mere broken torso . . . people will never learn what war means . . . [*he looks fearfully at one of the cripples, takes a step towards him, still talking to himself*]. Shall I ask my neighbour if the war is over . . .

THE OTHER CRIPPLE: *noticing the approach, suddenly angry and scared*] Just don't come too close . . . I don't like people . . . you can never be sure they don't have some dirty trick up their sleeves.

FIRST CRIPPLE: I too have only got one eye . . . and only one arm . . .

THE OTHER CRIPPLE: *afraid*] By the bright morning star, which still follows its accustomed path . . . I was a very peaceful man . . . I grazed my sheep peacefully on the clover stubble . . . and on the meadow . . . I was a very experienced, peace-loving shepherd . . . hahahaha . . . and suddenly I have a bayonet in my back . . . and don't even know who knocked me into the green grass . . . a couple of men in uniform had come up from behind the gully . . . and said I was their enemy . . . and there I lay . . . till the long night broke over me and now it is true I have awakened again out of the eternal darkness . . . but I do not trust . . .

FIRST CRIPPLE: Who are you then . . .

THE OTHER CRIPPLE: Who should I be . . . save the man you see before you . . . yes . . . Man and Beast are on their own . . . neither can trust the other . . .

FIRST CRIPPLE: You must have had a name sometime . . .

THE OTHER CRIPPLE: *meanwhile the cripples probing around with sticks in the fields increase from all quarters*] Yes, yes . . . I did have a name . . . but I don't have one any more . . . just don't come so close . . . you might want to convince me you were once an Emperor . . . or a General perhaps . . . or maybe only a General Manager . . . and were perhaps in a position to dismiss me from further service on this earth . . . that is not possible any more today, because since this great murderous business . . . [*the light in the sky towards the east grows very slowly*].

OTHER CRIPPLE: That is the place where the sun will perhaps be born again anew . . .

A few cripples follow each other around which has brought them close to the two cripples, digging.

ONE CRIPPLE: *formerly a philosopher*] There's the gleaming white uniform of a cavalryman.

64

OTHER CRIPPLE: *formerly a smith*] He is still stretching his hand out of the grave . . . with two rings on it.

PHILOSOPHER: I'll take them off . . . ah . . . a magnificent ruby . . . how it sparkles . . . perhaps dawn will break again, if the morning light is growing like that . . . oh . . . the play of the colours is like roses . . . I wager that was a present from his wife . . . he was a Colonel of Hussars . . . he has a diamond on his finger too . . . big as a . . . hah . . . how it sparkles . . . almost sure to have been a present from his beloved daughter . . .

SMITH: *looks him up and down secretly and suspiciously as he looks at the looted rings in his hand*] Hahahaha . . . a cripple . . . who gets sentimental . . . after the limbs have been torn from his body and one eye socket has been radically emptied . . . hahahaha . . . where do you get your fairy-tales from . . .

PHILOSOPHER: Where . . . hahahaha . . . where do I get my fairy-tales from . . . [*His senseless laughter changes to tears*]. My tears flow . . . I'll put these rings quietly on my fingers . . . for I do have some things to remember . . . some wonderful things . . . ah . . . some quite wonderful things . . . the war has killed off all that . . .

SMITH: *goes up closer to him and looks at him more and more curiously*] What were you then?

PHILOSOPHER: I was a man who had a wife and child and lived in a peaceful home . . . for instance, like this one here . . . no—this must have been a very distinguished palace . . . these are ruins of a very distinguished palace . . . of which the war has not left very much . . . this portal . . . ah . . . I wager one of the Princes of the Great Powers lived here . . . with his proud commanding voice . . . but the war has razed it all to the ground . . . his palace and my home which lay so peacefully among the hills outside the city . . . all razed to the ground . . .

SMITH: What did you do in the old days?

PHILOSOPHER: What should a man do who lives among peaceful hills?

SMITH: You keep talking round the point . . . I don't want to know your name, I don't even want to know who you once were . . . but I can tell from looking at you that you never swung a smith's hammer . . . you can still tell somebody who used to swing a smith's hammer just by looking at the stump of the arm and the mighty power that was in the muscles . . . you are a very refined . . . very gentle type . . . I bet the war really terrified you . . .

PHILOSOPHER: Me . . . you . . . everybody . . . even the insects crawling in the grass . . . even the worms crawling in the wood were terrified by the war—the timbers of houses groaned and cracked . . . the walls disintegrated . . . the tiles of the tiniest hut rattled down . . . even the birds that sat in the twigs were terrified by the war . . . everybody was in mortal terror of the war . . . those men whose duty did not force them to slaughter others, knelt and prayed incessantly: 'Holy God, God Almighty' even the leaves in the trees were in terror . . . the clouds swept across the sky like galloping horses . . . all the great trees in the forests trembled, as if they were to be uprooted . . . only one did not tremble . . . the Lord of War did not tremble . . . and something else did not tremble . . . my soul within me did not tremble . . . no tumult of war reaches my soul.

SMITH: *while a group of cripples gathers round the two of them, each new arrival approaching slowly, timidly and secretly examining the others and listening to their conversation*] You really do talk round and round the point . . . come on, tell us once and for all what you did . . . I mean what your job was before . . . if you don't want to tell me your name . . . and don't trust my words . . .

PHILOSOPHER: If one could trust you . . .

SMITH: Why not . . . do you think, because the war has chopped me up too into several halves . . . and one of my arms and one of my eyes are already mouldering in the grave . . .

PHILOSOPHER: *smiling childlike*] If one could trust now . . . oh, I so long for someone I could trust . . . I hunger so for someone I could trust . . .

SMITH: Yes . . . my God . . . TRUST . . . who could solve that puzzle for us . . .

PHILOSOPHER: *laughing childlike*] Hahahaha . . . you see I was once a Professor of Philosophy . . . I had written the most famous books . . . but now all philosophy is finished.

SMITH: And it looks as if the sun is going to rise again . . . brother . . .

PHILOSOPHER: Even with a word like brother you have to be very careful on such ground . . . brothers who tore each other to shreds lie here in thousands.

SMITH: Hahahaha . . . we can't carry a rifle any more . . .

PHILOSOPHER: Tell me one thing . . . is the war really over . . .

SMITH: Yes . . . the war is over . . .

ANOTHER: *calls across the field from a distance*] Be quiet for a minute . . . it is so wonderfully peaceful everywhere . . . tell me . . . is the war over . . .

OTHER VOICES: *solemnly*] Yes . . . the war is over . . .

ANOTHER: Can anybody say for sure?

ANOTHER: Yes, the war is over . . . there are only cripples and ruins left everywhere . . . here and there on earth a lonely hut stands spared . . . but in the cities nothing but the dogs chasing the rats . . . there are hordes of those bald-tailed rodents there . . . and where the corpses have not been eaten by the vultures the air is filled with the smell of decaying flesh . . . but if perhaps the sun did rise anew out of the night, it will all dry out quickly . . . and the mouldering flesh still lying around . . . even the crows have grown accustomed to eating human flesh . . .

SMITH: *in the group*] Yes . . . the war is over . . .

THE OTHER: *from a distance*] Yes . . . the war is over . . .

ANOTHER: *from a distance*] What are you all putting your heads together for before it is morning . . . what crazy new schemes are you thinking of breeding . . . hahahaha . . . what kind of cock and bull stories are you telling each other . . . come on . . . we're better off digging up the lost splendour of the old world . . .

PHILOSOPHER: *timidly*] Cynicism springing up anew.

A CRIPPLE: *from the group suddenly explodes into mad laughter*] You are still trying to soften up each other . . . so that you can believe in your crazy fantasies again, so that you can believe in salvation . . . [*he runs laughing and leaping to the cripples further away and there immediately joins in the digging*].

SMITH: Oh . . . don't be afraid . . . I can still swing my hammer with my left hand . . .

PHILOSOPHER: *while all look tensely at the cripples sneering from a distance*] Let's go behind the statue . . . you see . . . if these cripples all come back . . . and if each one of them has found some old treasure, they will grin at each other . . . and the spark of hatred will glimmer anew in them . . . for man is a wolf . . . he leads a greedy life as long as he has even one tooth left . . .

SMITH: And yet you once believed . . .

PHILOSOPHER: I had to teach the most remarkable things . . . you see I taught moral philosophy.

CRIPPLE: *in an old black morning coat without shoes and an old top hat, who has been standing with the group all the time. Very humbly*] You too . . . something so very sublime . . .

PHILOSOPHER: Yes, I taught philosophy . . . the philosophy of peace . . . with gentle voice . . . clean hands . . . with completely refined, noble presentation . . . I was illuminated . . . tongues of fire round my head . . . oh, I proclaimed ideas . . . the brave boys in front of me all thought, now at last the world had found release from the old murderous curse of WAR . . .

SMITH: *exploding in rage*] Thunder like mountain forests . . . like when the primeval storm hurls about a million pine trees bodily . . . that's how one should speak . . . not with the breath of man . . . mercilessly like God himself . . .

CRIPPLE: *in morning coat, quite gently*] Well, well, you too . . . something so very sublime . . .

SMITH: *again, with great excitement*] Angrily . . . violently . . . violently . . . mercilessly . . . like God himself . . . when he suddenly flings mountains playfully into the air and crushes 30,000 human beings like this in his hand . . .

PHILOSOPHER: So the war came . . . and in the end silenced even the human wolves . . . [*All suddenly look shamefacedly to the ground, and a deep silence comes over them*].

CRIPPLE: *in morning coat, very timidly and kindly*] Yes . . . yes . . . yes . . . the war has silenced even the human wolves . . . perhaps it has even slain the God within me with its hammers and killed Him with its sly bullet . . . or has the war not yet really filled in my pure spring . . . yes . . . [*He turns round to take a few steps*]. If only I knew of a meadow here or a swamp where reeds grow . . . you see I was a musician in the Cathedral Orchestra which always played to the glory of God . . . there I'll cut a simple little reed flute . . . and I want at least to try to play a sweet song for mankind again . . . [*He turns back to the group casually and says with gentle self-irony and a humble laugh*]. Vanyka the Good made a whole herd of wild pigs, including the wild boar, dance to his flute . . . and the flute-player from the Nile enticed the sharp-toothed crocodiles from the water with his sweet playing . . . so that even that vicious brood modified its hateful habits for a short time . . . just to listen to the gentle song . . .

SMITH: You too killed your brother . . .

PHILOSOPHER: I too . . .

CRIPPLE: *in morning coat*] Yes . . . I too . . .

PHILOSOPHER: Are you French . . . or . . . something else . . .

SMITH: A Frenchman . . . and you . . . do you too belong to some former race? . . .

PHILOSOPHER: I am a German . . .

CRIPPLE: *in morning coat*] Oh, my God . . . of course we can't embrace . . . but I can touch you tenderly with my lips . . . for my soul hungers for your soul . . . that the light of humanity may burn in us again with its thousand tears . . . and grow again . . . Faith . . . Trust . . .

SMITH: *as* CRIPPLE *in morning coat kisses him too*] So you are not afraid to kiss the old wolf in us.

CRIPPLE *in morning coat wanders away lost in thought.*

CRIPPLE: *with an old sack over his shoulder, a stick in his hand, a bandaged stump of a foot, arrives singing and laughing*]

O, the world is fair,
When the lilac blooms,
When the beech twig beams from the bough.

Haha . . . I used to be a rag-and-bone man . . . and I still am . . . hahaha . . . when you look at where you are in the prime of your life . . . and look at the rags on your stump of a foot . . . hahaha . . . then it is easy to convince yourself that the world has really driven you into a corner . . . but that shouldn't make you weep and moan all the time, my fellow-cripples . . . hahahaha . . . I used to have a hay waggon full of love affairs . . . now I live solo in a miserable hole in the ground . . . Thank God . . . and when I lay me down to die and close my eyes forever . . . the flesh off my body can find the path to the sun again bit by bit in the stomach of a vulture . . . that's as much as any fleshy mortal excretion can ask for, isn't it . . . take a look here . . . I've accumulated the craziest things in my rag-bag . . . Lady's Ceremonial Dress . . . only to be worn on Court occasions . . . here a grey pearl in a white stiff shirt front even . . . I bet it is the famous pearl Julius Caesar once gave to Servilia . . . or the pearl of Abdul Hamid . . . or the pearl of Venice, that Sultan Soliman received as a present . . . in my little hole in the ground I shall open a museum of valuable antiquities . . . my fellow cripples . . . and engage a Professor to identify and explain the excavated treasures thoroughly . . . [*Assumes the posture of a lecturer*]. Most esteemed ladies and gentlemen . . . hahahaha . . . the wonderful old days . . . of which only a few comical cripples have been left over . . . that heroic age . . . that great sublime age, when men lived in bold conflicts, as long as they bore the sword in their hands . . . till these swords fell from their hands . . . taking the hand and most of the arm with it . . . hahahahaha . . . [*Song*].

> The man who sang this song to me,
> Was as quick as a trick with a sword . . .
> In the day-time he'd swing it merrily;
> Sing at night of the battles he'd fought . . .

Singing this song he hobbles over to his bolt-hole and crawls into it. Now and then other cripples carry what they have gathered in sacks into their bolt-holes.

ONE OF THE CRIPPLES: *who has been standing some way off, suddenly raises a strange cry*] Horriduh, horriduh, horriduh . . . [*All the cripples look up. The group gives a start. Out of the group speaks the*] SMITH: Is there suddenly some happy news?

PHILOSOPHER: Morning is climbing up the sky.

CRIPPLE: *in morning coat, calls from a distance—he is busy cutting himself a flute*] Yes, morning is climbing up the sky.

GRUSCHKA: *has appeared out of the distance. She has a child at her breast. She talks to the child*] No, no, no, no . . . I have to shield your young eyes from the light my child . . . if dawn breaks now . . . [*She covers the child with a fine little blanket, and walks like a loving mother, with eyes for the child alone, as if she were not merely sheltering it in her arms, but also with her eyes*].

CRIPPLE: *stands as if he has seen game*] Ah . . . a woman [*He throws his mattock away*] Tally-ho—the hunt is on [*He leaps at* GRUSCHKA *lustfully*].

A FEW CRIPPLES: *from various directions holding him back and shouting confusedly*] Swine . . . filthy wretch . . . stop . . . filthy swine. . . .

ANOTHER CRIPPLE: Horriduh . . . horriduh . . . horriduh . . .

Movement comes into the other cripples too. They follow GRUSCHKA *with their eyes, one after the other tears a green shoot from the ground or a bush and begins hesitantly to follow her.* GRUSCHKA *strides slowly to the chapel.* CRIPPLE *in the morning coat tries a little pastorale on his flute in the distance.*

ONE OF THE CRIPPLES: It is a woman bearing a child in her arms . . . it is a mother . . .

FATHER FRANCIS *who has sat down tiredly on a tree trunk—lying in the little temple and fallen asleep after completing the simple construction, wakens with the joyful life approaching and stands upright in the temple.*

A CRIPPLE: *calls*] She is carrying a baby boy in her arms . . .
ANOTHER: Just look . . . a little temple has arisen there and spring has grown out of the earth overnight.
ANOTHER: *calls*] The woman is carrying the child to Father Francis.

The MERRY CRIPPLE *has stuck his head out of his bolt-hole, comes out expectantly and looks out over the morning meadow. He approaches the chapel too and picks up a twig on the way which he weaves into a wreath and puts in his hair.*

MERRY CRIPPLE: *laughing gaily*] Hahahaha . . . it will be a little boy again . . . that's the funny thing . . . same old tread-mill

. . . the woman has received a man's seed . . . and now the son of man lies there, still in his swaddling clothes . . . it is true my fine cripples . . . but who can tell whether he might not grow up to become a General . . . hahahaha . . .

While all the cripples press hesitantly forward to the chapel a second young woman like GRUSCHKA *lost in contemplation of the child in her arms comes striding along from the distance.*

CRIPPLES: *call*] War lies sleeping . . .
OTHERS: *call*] The cruel blood has seeped away.

Immediately behind the second, far off there appears a third young woman with a child in her arms, the same posture, coming the same way. As GRUSCHKA *approaches the steps* FATHER FRANCIS *has opened his arms to receive her; he comes down a few steps to meet her.*

GRUSCHKA: *stops before the steps, looks down at the child again tenderly and says*] Oh, Father Francis . . . just look . . . the little boy Enoch . . . he has sprung from my blood . . . [*she caresses him with her hand*]. Enoch . . . Enoch . . . you still have to protect his young eyes from the sun. Father . . . how he blinks . . . the new dawn has come, oh Lord, out of the goodness of your rich, good heart let your great love for this poor lovely earth spill over into the blood of this sweet boy . . . he is my Enoch . . .
SOME OF THE CRIPPLES: *somehow adorned with greenery, grouped round the chapel, cry with passionate joy*] Enoch . . . it is Enoch . . .
OTHERS: *call in joyful confusion*] Horriduh . . . Horriduh . . . Horriduh . . .
ANOTHER: *calls*] Oh Lord . . . your great love for this poor lovely earth . . .
OTHERS: *call*] He is Cain's son.
OTHERS: *call*] The son of Cain, the murderer of his brother.
IN GREAT CONFUSED CHORUS: He is Cain's son—Enoch.

The pastorale of the lonely flute joins in vigorously, while amid general rejoicing the whole stage sinks into darkness.

NAVAL ENCOUNTER
Reinhard Goering

1917

Translated by J. M. Ritchie and J. D. Stowell

NAVAL ENCOUNTER

Those taking part are seven sailors, going into action in the gunturret of a warship. As the curtain rises, the first, second, fourth and sixth are in the turret, the sixth furthest towards the back. The play opens with a cry.

FIRST SAILOR: A sign! A sign!

SECOND SAILOR: What's he shouting? What rubbish is that he's shouting?

THE FIRST: A sign! A sign! Of when we'll strike them and what the outcome will be.

THE SECOND: You old fool! Where's this sign to be?

THE FIRST: A sign in the blue sky. Of when we'll strike them and what the outcome will be.

THE SECOND: You old fool! Be content to see nothing but blue in the blue of the sky! A man sailing with us once, he saw signs in the blue sky. Sitting behind bars today! He sang, sang behind bars: 'O blue of the sky! O blue of the sky! My eyes roam over you like nomads in the desert and die—of thirst'. A sorry sound. We laughed.

THE FOURTH: Laughing ought to put you behind bars too.

THE SECOND: A sorry sound. We laughed. Is laughing such a terrible thing? We've notched up a lot of laughter, so we must be great sinners. I suppose weeping is better?

THE FOURTH: Weeping—if there's still such a thing as tears —ought to be punished.

THE SECOND: And what rewarded?

THE FOURTH: Nothing.

THE FIRST: But once it becomes clear what the higher powers want of us—

THE SECOND: Oh, no! You're not on about that again, mate? Where did the higher powers ever get you? How long would they keep you going? The way they teach children's lips to lisp lies about higher powers, until the bitter mouths scream, because they are on their own! They make eyes lose confidence in what they can see for themselves! And make them look backwards

75

like toads! Not a day is made bright by higher powers. Or, friend, standing there at the gunbarrel, have you ever seen something aiming from outside, unknown, sailing under other colours, with ghoulish fingers and ghostly gleam across the sea? Have you ever seen such a thing? Old wives' tales! Tug of the forelock from men with no guts! Don't be taken in by it.

THE FIRST: You won't deny a man can have a feeling there's something inside us giving us signs that tell of things to come.

THE SECOND: Just be quiet a minute, lad! Do you hear singing? Call it throbbing if you like. Throbbing that never lets up! Take a look! Don't you like the play of these mountings, smooth, soundless, cat-like and patient? This gunbarrel, a real thoroughbred, tended like an empress! These are the signs that tell you what will happen to us. That, and these cursed bodies here, and everything in them fed on blood. If we had nothing more on board than what you say, and put your faith in, I tell you straight: We are pigs on our way to the slaughter. But this is as boring as a Sunday sermon! Can you dance? Or at least could you? Are you a dancer too? What more do you want than dancing and sleeping! Action? Don't they call that the 'hot dance'? Sleep! Isn't that all death is? Sing your head off, that's the best thing! Isn't today the last day of May? If we were on land waiting for nightfall, instead of here at sea, waiting for the enemy, there'd be a merry dance tonight! Wouldn't there? Of course there would!

He sings.

THE FIRST: With quiet lights something slips away over our heads. I can't tell you more, it comes from lands without measure. Do you call that nothing? Don't you believe in second sight? Oh, why must I be so weak today that I speak!

THE FOURTH: Is he still on about signs?

THE SECOND: It's second sight now.

THE FOURTH: Second sight! Morning mists of the brain! Women and children are wreathed in them. Once sun sweeps manhood up to its peak such things become no more than an evil fog in the world's clear blue.

THE SECOND: What do you see in the future, lad? Give us a look!

76

THE FIRST: That this time we'll strike them, and that none shall return.

THE FOURTH: Hoho! You forecast after the storm! We're all, all of us here, well and truly drowned. And what if it is today? How can you tell? What's the use of wanting to know? If it's coming, it's coming. You've got your head all stuffed with fairy-stories. You'd think a man would get sick of fairy-stories.

THE SECOND: Listen to him! But it's not fear that gives you second sight, is it? You're not afraid, are you? Eh?

THE FIRST: If we are to be called away today, there is not much time to get ready.

THE SECOND: This fellow is not of our time. Has he been talking like this for long? You probably haven't ever done much kissing; so now you're sorry about the rose-buds you missed, now you learn too late they're for plucking!

THE SIXTH: Four o'clock, Do you hear, lads? We should get some sleep. Sleep so we have strength when the shooting starts. Stretch out, lads.

The THIRD SAILOR *enters.*

THE THIRD: Bets. We strike them! Any bets, we strike them? The day's half gone. Any bets we strike them before it's over?

THE SECOND: Strike who?

THE THIRD: Ships! You donkey!

THE SECOND: Ha ha! Laugh! Never saw him as hot as this except looking for girls. He's got some in every port. You've got that longing look, lad!

THE THIRD: Ships! Ships!

THE SECOND: Malayan embraces, that last a bare two minutes, till the siren sounds again; no prayer and no ceremony; just action: he's got a cooler head on him then, I can tell you. Phew, just look at him!

THE THIRD: Ships! Ships!

THE SECOND: Master of harbour love bred in brothels.

THE THIRD: Ships! Ships! Let me call flesh a fire that burns and burns. I'll stay on board, bashful and alone, when the anchor-chains rattle down in distant ports, I'll do everything you want. But just let me taste battle, the fight, the test, the trial of who's the better seamen, us or them.

THE SECOND: Patience, lad.

THE THIRD: Patience is for the birds! The world is too patient these days! Patience is no mark of beauty.

THE FIRST: Patience itself is beautiful.

THE THIRD: Ships! Ships! Waiting, inactivity: that's a poison that eats into men faster than pent-up lust.

THE SECOND: Patience! Somebody here says we'll strike them today and there'll be action.

THE THIRD: Who? Him? How does he know?

THE SECOND: Heard it from his aunty, who's always warning him about the wicked month of May.

THE FIRST: Coarse lot! Haven't I taken my share of the watch here on the water, and stared over the sea day and night? And longed for action like you? Far, far away I saw smoke of ships, little wisps. Could be enemy. If it was; I talked like you. But my eyes played me no tricks. Nobody can say of me that I saw too soon or called too quick. Why do you laugh at me? Wait! You'll learn a lot before night falls!

THE THIRD: We'll learn no more! Bet my life. What more would there be to learn!

THE SECOND: You'll see, we'll know how to drown when we have to, just as if we'd been trained. We'll know how to let our eyes, shining with the glory of youth, sink into the salt sea spray, no need for salt tears then.

THE THIRD: So, ships! We can look after the rest for ourselves.

THE SECOND: Freedom of the sea! Freedom of the sea! Won't even you be pleased, won't it be something to be proud of, when the sea, caressing the sand on summer nights, sings hymns of praise to us as liberators, or the wave roars with our deeds at the sullen cliff. As long as wave shall roll.

THE SIXTH: Sleep, men! Sleep! You'll soon be needed again.

THE FOURTH: All this heat makes you soft. When ships come, when the first eye picks them out and then the news leaps from man to man, when keels cleave, gunbarrels swivel, battle roars, naked men leap in mountains of coal and all groans under action: then tell me—what more is there to it than us just doing the job we're supposed to? What is so different?

THE THIRD: Are you asking us that?

THE FOURTH: Yes, you!

THE THIRD: Hell and damnation, when the battle breaks loose, trial of strength, in earnest, test of who is the better seamen, when we see if we are what we think we are; when game turns to earnest, truth is revealed: he calls that: no difference!

THE FOURTH: I call that: no difference.

THE THIRD: And you? And you? And you?

THE SECOND: I think everything'll be different, if battle breaks out the way he foresees.

THE FOURTH: And for me: no matter what happens, for real men nothing is different.

THE SIXTH: It's nearly half-past four. Sleep, men! Sleep! You'll soon be needed again.

THE THIRD: We must sleep now.

THE SECOND: Early to bed! Our beds are sheets of steel, with a hollow for every head.

THE FOURTH: How is the sea running?

THE SECOND: Silent. Calm! Like a flock of sheep. Caressed by Nor' West wind. A day for taking girls for a sail, it would be. We passed Sylt a while ago. That fine, blonde island was never kissed by gentler wave.

THE FOURTH: Did you see sentries on the shore?

THE SECOND: Everywhere, And alert! They saw us pass. Their hearts follow after us, with envy.

THE FOURTH: Envy, do you say? Do you really think envy?

THE SIXTH: Sleep. Time's running out! We'll soon be needed again.

THE SECOND: See how he's got his arm round his gunbarrel already! As if he were dreaming up Samoa. How would it be, lad, if you gave us a yarn about Samoa to send us off to sleep. How love makes fools of chaste northerners there.

THE THIRD: Samoa! Island! Shall I tell you quickly then? Just promise me this: if death comes for me, shout that name once more in my ear!

THE SECOND: Good, we promise.

THE THIRD: Oh, ha ha, Samoa! When we first landed there, it was like a new dawn, like being drunk. Blokes were bawling in the sunshine and calling their own country indifferent, stupid, cold, hopeless. Swore they'd never again be able to breathe properly at home. What do you want to know? Our fathers were mad never to go there, and bastards not to have spawned us there!

We were there three days. And we all felt as if we had been madmen till then, mules lumping the rubbish and troubles of others, useless ballast, self-inflicted torture. [*The* FIFTH SAILOR *enters and goes into a corner without taking notice of anybody, and sits down*]. Here he comes just at the right moment. Come here, lad, and tell them about Samoa. You were there, weren't you? If they start shouting: I'm lying, you pipe up: It's true. D'ye hear? Eh? Not talking? Dumb's a wall? Not even a hullo?

THE FOURTH: Let him sleep! He's just come off third watch.

THE THIRD: Listen, lad, we're talking about Samoa.

THE SECOND: Leave him be. Go on with your story.

THE THIRD: The women there! We called them date-plants! And did we plant dates! One time—without a word of lie—we came into a village. Two weeks we were there. And we really knew we were living. What we'd seen till then was miserable. They were a friendly lot there, had funny customs. Like, they said: Life's short. Don't make it harder than it is! Don't make life a misery! A man would rather hang himself than take anything amiss. Women always went round in pairs and two counted as one. Not a word of a lie. They were quick and bright little things. Always ready to help. And we never saw one pull a face. We planted dates there all right—as often as we were able.

THE SECOND: Big mouth! What a pack of lies. Trying to give us bad dreams.

THE FOURTH: At sea, anyone who can make us dream of something besides battle can lie as much as he likes.

THE THIRD: Somebody say I'm lying? Ask that sleepy character behind me there. Ask him!

THE FOURTH: Quiet. He's asleep already.

THE SECOND: He's still got his eyes wide open. Wider than a fish. Like the church warden pretending he's praying.

THE THIRD: Ask him.

THE SECOND: Hey, lad!

THE THIRD: No answer.

THE FOURTH: You should let him sleep.

THE THIRD: Hold on! Haven't I seen him like that before? When there was a really nice piece in a port somewhere, when all you could see in his eye was her hitched-up skirt, the loose bit of stocking, the dress cut so low the hair on your neck bristles, that's exactly the look he had then. Eyed her as if glued to the spot. Went no closer. Stood still as a post. Suddenly remembers he's got something to do on board and beats it. That's how he was. Hey there, m'lad!

THE SECOND: Doesn't hear.

THE FIRST: Listening to other voices than yours.

THE SECOND: Won't hear much then.

THE FIRST: Or thinking of mother, friend or fiancée.

THE SECOND: We've got mothers too, and friends, and fiancées as well, of a sort. As many as we like. Still hear, though, when somebody calls and says hullo.

THE THIRD: What's the good of crying for mother. Enough when they cry for us. From commodore to cook, there's only one thought now and that's the one he's got: watch me make him jump. Hey! Ships! Enemy ships!

THE SECOND: There's a lad here with a feeling today's the day. We're to learn a lot and then go to the bottom. It's written in the blue sky.

THE FOURTH: Noisy bastards, can't you leave the man in peace, he stood two watches for you.

THE FIRST: Maybe he sees what we can't; what's going on inside his head we keep below the surface.

THE SECOND: There are queer birds like that. But he's not one of them.

THE FIRST: How do you know that?

THE SECOND: He's laughing the whole day. He enjoys life like the rest of us.

THE THIRD: Let's wake him up. By all the lovely days we had and the lovelier ones to come, what's got into you, lad? Do you want to do something, and you can't make up your mind? Seize it by the throat! Don't chew it over too much. Don't wait for the O.K. Grab the bull by the horns! Do you want to go to sleep? Right, shut your eyes! First one and then the other! Else we'll get the shivers. Eyes must have sparkle, or you can't face food.

THE FOURTH: Half-past four! Time's really up and I'm giving the order. Everybody sleep and no more talk! That's an order.

THE THIRD: This little trip won't come to anything either. Stuff this for a life!

THE SECOND: At least we've learned something this time: how to read the blue of the sky, and that there are people who stare into space, hear nothing and can't even say 'Good-day'.

The men lie down and take up sleeping positions. The FIFTH SAILOR *after a time starts moving his arms about.*

THE SECOND: Damn! Now he's going to start getting jumpy.
THE THIRD: Let him jump and kick. Can't help him.
THE SECOND: Grappling with ghosts.
THE THIRD: Doesn't make much noise.
THE SECOND: Brushing flies from his eyes.
THE THIRD: None troubling us. Perhaps he can see little people too, like the fellow who saw men walking across the water.
THE SECOND: Sick, then?
THE THIRD: None of our business now.
THE FIRST: Stubborn lot you are! Hard lot! I'm amazed.
THE THIRD: Nothing amazes us. First step to manhood. Better to listen to the waves now. Rock-a-bye baby. Nothing amazes the waves either. Do you hear?
THE FIRST: Mad lot, you are!
THE THIRD: We don't fuss. That's all. When you get the habit too you'll get on better. Rock-a-bye baby, listen to the waves. They don't fuss either.

They then settle down to sleep again. After a while the FIFTH SAILOR *starts muttering.*

THE SECOND: God help us, if he isn't starting to preach.
THE THIRD: We'll sleep all the better for it.
THE SECOND: Just take a look at him. Listen to him though.
THE THIRD: Why so solemn? What's the matter with him?

They listen for a while to the muttering of the FIFTH SAILOR, *then the* THIRD SAILOR *stands up.*

THE THIRD: Bo's'n, sorry for what I am about to say! But it must be said. There's a man here on board who is afraid of dying. Do you want to know where he's sitting? There! Sorry, bo's'n, but I'm forced to say it. I accuse no man without reason. The man is afraid of Death. That's what.

82

THE FOURTH: Fear of Death is a myth these days.

THE THIRD: I just heard him muttering: Death, Death; that's all. He doesn't want action at sea, he'd rather go home, he's muttering Death, Death, Death.

THE FOURTH: There's no such thing as Fear of Death any more.

THE SECOND: Anybody who had it, has forgotten what it was.

THE FOURTH: One word! He can't mean anything by it.

THE THIRD: One thing is certain. There's no room for him here. Or are we to have somebody in here, who will die of fright on us before the first shot is fired?

THE FOURTH: Rubbish. Nobody does that.

THE THIRD: What are you going to do with him?

THE FOURTH: What am I going to do with him? With him? Nothing.

THE SECOND: That's not much.

THE THIRD: With the fear that's inside his head?

THE FOURTH: Doesn't matter what's inside your head. That's not what counts.

THE SECOND: He's sick, I said.

THE FOURTH: We know that sickness. Soon as the banging starts, it's cured. Don't make so much of it, lads. Is he the first to go down with it? Just the same for anyone who can't stand the waiting.

THE THIRD: Him just being in here is an insult.

THE FOURTH: Don't take yourselves so seriously, mates! Or you'll be beginners all your life.

THE THIRD: That man must go! Are you with me? Let's get him out.

THE FOURTH: Take it easy. Don't be too hasty. Just a moment. I'm the one who gives the orders: I think so anyway. Lie down and sleep. That's an order. And once and for all: Quiet. And you: just wait: you'll be sorry.

THE THIRD: Sorry! That'll be the day.

THE FOURTH: What's the time?

THE SECOND: Quarter to five. We must be close to the Skagerrak now. The sea is quiet. Just the occasional clap of a wave.

THE FIRST: Soon many a glassy man will rise from the sea in the land of the Jutes.

THE SECOND: Glassy man? What are you babbling about.

THE FIRST: Soon many a glassy man will rise from the sea in the land of the Jutes.

The men now fall asleep. The muttering of the FIFTH SAILOR *begins again and becomes intelligible.*

THE FIFTH: What to do? It's like when mosquitoes won't let you sleep. The quieter you lie, the louder they whine. Once one finds the way, thousands follow. Maybe better to let yourself be bitten than thresh about so much! My father and his father never had this experience. They only had thoughts that were some use to them. Their brain was to them what the nose is to a dog. They went by instinct. Nowadays there are swarms with a thousand stings around our heads. If there's blood, it turns bad in the skull, like water in an old sponge. The bubbles from it may shine with all the colours, but it's putrefaction. Bubble or light: that's what counts. Away across the sea, in the night, to the waves, where your brother or sister sits rocking, beyond grasp, beyond reach, so that we dream, when we look long in that direction. Flower quite new? Who saw it grow? World trots still to that same stable? But there is something hanging between us, that attacks suddenly as plague strikes peasant and master: better then crawl to a hole, stop ears, scream: Not me, not me! Before you go down with it. Are we not saddled with articles of belief of a leather to outlast all wind and water?

The sleeping sailors have begun to dream and now interrupt the FIFTH.

THE SECOND: My arm? Let go!
THE THIRD: My knee? Get down!
THE SECOND: Nothing.
THE THIRD: See any wisps of smoke?
THE SECOND: Wisps of smoke? Give every man an extra ration. Help yourself. Gulp it down. Guts it.
THE THIRD: What are they feeding us up for?
THE SECOND: Guts it! Is it good? Guts it!
THE THIRD: Got no taste.
THE SECOND: Wipe all the muck off the deck.
THE THIRD: Nothing.

84

THE SECOND: See any wisps of smoke?
THE FOURTH: Not sleeping. Can't sleep. Help me sleep, somebody!

SECOND SAILOR *half-raises himself.*

THE SECOND: Not yet?

Sinks back again; the THIRD *follows his action.*

THE THIRD: Not yet?
THE SECOND: When will the waiting be over?
THE FOURTH: I can't sleep. Help me sleep, somebody.

The men are silent again, but continue to make movements.

THE FIFTH: Your dream? Yes. Mine too? Are you getting worked up, mates? Lay down your heads again! Seamen's blood rising and falling, sudden like the sea. Why do you jerk and twitch? What is your will? Action. Three times into action, without why or wherefore. Just on with it. Action! Lay down your heads again.

The FIFTH SAILOR *steps up to the* FOURTH.

THE FIFTH: And this man wants somebody to help him sleep. And aren't you asleep? A dead man wouldn't sleep sounder. And still he cries: Give me sleep?

The FIFTH SAILOR *steps up to the* FIRST.

THE FIFTH: But this one! Doesn't say a word? Sleeps! As much as to say: I'm safe. Sleep soundly! Sleep sweet.

He walks away.

THE FIFTH: Sleep on, all of you. For one man keeps watch here. If he were to sleep now, it would be sheer funk.

The FIRST SAILOR *stands up, steps behind the* FIFTH *and rests his hands on his shoulder.*

THE FIRST: I'm not asleep either, mate.
THE FIFTH: Ghost!

THE FIRST: Sorry if I frightened you.

THE FIFTH: Hell and damnation, a ghost couldn't have got up quieter and groaned as hollow as you just now. What do you want?

THE FIRST: Just to tell you I wasn't sleeping.

THE FIFTH: Acted as if you were, though. Did look as if you were sleeping very sweetly. Putting it on, then? What game are you up to with me now? Speak up.

THE FIRST: No game, comrade.

THE FIFTH: The way he says that: No game. What do you want, then? Why aren't you sleeping?

THE FIRST: Seemed to me just now, as if I were listening to an invocation. As if you were calling on some spirits or other, or higher powers.

THE FIFTH: Wrong, completely wrong. I was calling on myself. I know nothing at all about higher powers. Anyone honouring them is putting himself on the string that makes a puppet of him.

THE FIRST: But we are all puppets.

THE FIFTH: Do you think so? Life in the raw, eh? Say no more, man.

THE FIRST: Glutton for punishment, aren't you?

THE FIFTH: Let it show, did I?

THE FIRST: Never any use.

THE FIFTH: Do you think so?

THE FIRST: Know it.

THE FIFTH: Well, what do you want?

THE FIRST: That's a mystery.

THE FIFTH: What could you do?

THE FIRST: There are things floating free in the air. When their time comes, they pass through any open window, regardless of who lives in the house. They pass, through closed windows too.

The FIFTH SAILOR *jumps back.*

THE FIFTH: That's the truth, boy.

THE FIRST: Is truth-telling a thing to cause fear?

THE FIFTH: Shouldn't be done.

THE FIRST: What did I say that's so terrible?

THE FIFTH: We two have said enough. Lie down again and sleep.
THE FIRST: I obey.

The FIRST SAILOR *goes and lies down again.*

THE FIFTH: Obeys! Now what's all this? I've no rights whatsoever over this man and yet he obeys me, calls it obeying. There are things floating free in the air, he says. Does he know them too? Hey, you there, comrade! Are you asleep again already? Come here, will you? Get up, there are things to be said. Time is on fire. We must separate smoke from fire. Time is a joker. We must seize the heart, throw away the shell, cut away the flaps and frills. Swim through the maelstrom, naked and free of vanity. So I will begin. Come!

The FIRST SAILOR *gets up again.*

THE FIRST: I come to your call, but well you know every man is for himself, whether willing or not.
THE FIFTH: I know nothing. Wait and see.
THE FIRST: What do you want of me, then?
THE FIFTH: Tell me straight what is in the air.
THE FIRST: You're asking the impossible.
THE FIFTH: Come! Speak freely. Nobody can hear us.
THE FIRST: You're asking the impossible, I tell you.
THE FIFTH: The way you came up just now, what you said, the way you lay down, the way you come again, all this fills me with expectation. Don't disappoint me.
THE FIRST: Maybe if we talked quite calmly and simply, after many words we would reach some goal.
THE FIFTH: Many words are not for me. Begin anyway!
THE FIRST: What's in the air, you ask me? Have you looked at the sea? It's there, too.
THE FIFTH: True, mate! True again!
THE FIRST: We've been travelling this sea for a long time now, water beneath and the skies above us. That makes a big difference.
THE FIFTH: This endless waste of water and eternal sky stirs up our souls and never lets us rest. The soul stands watch when it stares at the waves and when the wind sings bleak in the rigging.

87

THE FIRST: When we test our schemes against such powers and our strength against forces that play with us.

THE FIFTH: What then, comrade?

THE FIRST: Aye, what?

THE FIFTH: You're slipping away from me again, mate. Take care! Can't you feel the turmoil inside me so I'm almost afraid to say more.

THE FIRST: Then we'd better break off, for what the hour bids us do is new to me too. On this road I am as a child.

THE FIFTH: Children walk sure, where grown-ups stumble. Let us be as two children, as two pilgrims in a mist, who want to lose neither each other nor the way. Let us speak.

THE FIRST: As you wish. Maybe we shall recognize by its effects what we cannot name directly, and then find words for it too. Listen, then. We have been ordered to sleep now. They obey as is their duty. Why are the two of us not sleeping?

THE FIFTH: Because we cannot sleep. Sure, we can be ordered to lie down like sleepers, but nobody has any power over sleep itself.

THE FIRST: And why can't we sleep?

THE FIFTH: Because something different keeps us awake.

THE FIRST: Different from what?

THE FIFTH: From the force driving these others to obey.

THE FIRST: And shouldn't we allow only that in our soul which will make us obedient?

THE FIFTH: You are right. We should.

THE FIRST: But it's our soul that refuses obedience, obsessed as it is with something different. It's not wish or desire makes us disobedient. But a nameless fate of the soul.

THE FIFTH: It is so. But pause here. Don't you, too, feel the chill of horror? Where can this lead us? Is it not better to stop now. Obey even now and lie down.

THE FIRST: Just as you think. As you wish.

THE FIFTH: Oh, man, do you think me a coward, not daring to press on, now we are in sight of a wonderful goal? I want us to continue, even if it should mean the worst for us.

THE FIRST: We are now climbers, accepting the risks and daring the highest peaks. Before we start, let us call upon those powers who guide our steps from above.

THE FIFTH: Stop, friend! No! You do that alone. This I believe to the marrow of my bones: in all spheres we rely on ourselves alone and only get as far as our own two feet will firmly carry us. I draw strength from this. Our fate lies within ourselves. I would rather believe that we are glass, playthings, puppets in the hand of a crazy giant, than that an Intelligence controls us from above.

THE FIRST: I have made my appeal. We can continue.

THE FIFTH: Terrible is the power of word and thought. One man or millions, they lead the right way or astray. We can do our best.

THE FIRST: Hold fast to the heart of life, and the power of thought is kind. It opens up to us our innermost being, as roads and canals do a rich land. We would be dead men without thought, and much is dead because the thought in it has never been given life.

THE FIFTH: Now answer me!

THE FIRST: What do you want to ask?

THE FIFTH: Nobody listening?

THE FIRST: All are asleep.

THE FIFTH: But not for much longer. We must be brief and use our time. We must do what our country commands, mustn't we?

THE FIRST: Of course.

THE FIFTH: For it is always good to do as our country commands?

THE FIRST: But we must do what it commands because we owe everything to it.

THE FIFTH: And what do the poorest of the poor owe it?

THE FIRST: Much, much more than there are words to tell.

THE FIFTH: Life is sweet and lovely. The sun tosses us golden days; Gay Abandon smiles from the woods. Love decks herself with flowers; Youth dances enraptured in the fields. A drum roll —and all is over! Life is no longer of value. One by one they answer the summons of Death. For two years the happy song has been silent. For two years we have roamed the waves, blind and obsessed, killing, dying. Nobody remembers anything else, nobody talks of anything else, there is nothing left but kill and be killed.

THE FIRST: If one's country commands, then it has to be done.

THE FIFTH: Dying is not so bad. But who are we and who were

89

we? Do you still see things with your own eyes? Do you know what seized hold of you?

THE FIRST: If one's country commands, then it has to be done.

THE FIFTH: Why does the country command this?

THE FIRST: Because it seems necessary.

THE FIFTH: Can madness not reign over a whole nation and sway even its leaders? Must we do the will of madmen?

THE FIRST: We must.

THE FIFTH: What are we fighting for now?

THE FIRST: For freedom of the sea.

THE FIFTH: So that's what your mother suckled you for. That's what you were made for, body and soul.

THE FIRST: Oh, no, my mother knew nothing of this, nor I.

THE FIFTH: And what did you find you were made for?

THE FIRST: This: to serve God.

THE FIFTH: Oh, no! Oh, no! You thrust me from the clouds! I fall. Our words had nearly led on to the right answer, step by step they were climbing higher and higher. I was beginning to think we could soon call it by name, and now you have flung me down to the depths! Where is your God? What other? Who is this man who always turns aside? We were near to the one goal that can be grasped, and you blunder past into even thicker haze.

THE FIRST: If only you knew God and His service!

THE FIFTH: If only you knew your self!

THE FIRST: Having Him, you have all.

THE FIFTH: Having self, you have all. Yet it's true I have sensed what is real, I doubt myself and I wonder if I'm sane. But am I mad, lunatic, raving, or are the rest of you, or is it the age? You shall be judge! That's why you were awake before, why you wakened with your words what I would perhaps have wreathed in sleep. That's why you're here now.

THE FIRST: Do you believe you can make me shift my ground?

THE FIFTH: Yes, I want to and I will.

THE FIRST: You want to break down what life and my years of suffering have cemented firm within me?

THE FIFTH: I will blow upon it and it shall fall!

THE FIRST: You are mad.

THE FIFTH: Listen!

THE FIRST: Speak!

THE FIFTH: Do you believe that human kind has achieved the ultimate possible between two individuals?

THE FIRST: Speak plainer so that I do not misunderstand.

THE FIFTH: You agree, there are matters between one person and another?

THE FIRST: Granted.

THE FIFTH: Do you think we know anything of these matters?

THE FIRST: Too much.

THE FIFTH: Listen to me, man: nothing. Is that not our most immediate concern? Your answer again.

THE FIRST: Most immediate, yes.

THE FIFTH: But to us still remote, more remote than the furthest stars. Name something which earns people praise.

THE FIRST: Power.

THE FIFTH: Power through power?

THE FIRST: Agreed.

THE FIFTH: And do you know any power that men yearn for as much as they hate power through power? The greater its sphere of influence, the greater the lust for more, and the greater the lust the bigger it grows. Name something else.

THE FIRST: Possession.

THE FIFTH: Do you know of any possession, inexhaustible in scope and depth, compared with which the infinite sum of the stars seems small?

THE FIRST: What are you driving at?

THE FIFTH: If you had the faintest inkling of what can join two mortal beings then you would feel as if we were arguing about heaps of sand, as if a heap of sand were not as blind as we.

THE FIRST: It's easy to speak of feeling. What about really knowing?

THE FIFTH: I know. I know. That's just it, I know it for sure.

THE FIRST: What are you so sure of?

THE FIFTH: This above all: that there is something in the bond between two individuals reduces all we do to madness. Whatever they say, whatever they say, our false leaders.

THE FIRST: You're trying once more to put the blame on those who lead us?

THE FIFTH: On them and ourselves and all time. We were cowards and had not the courage to see or hear.

THE FIRST: This is what you say now!

THE FIFTH: Oh, I know what we are doing is madness and crime, and this is the only reason why: there is a certain bond between man and man; obeying it is a more sacred duty than any other.

THE FIRST: And how do you know that?

THE FIFTH: I know it. And I'm not the only one.

THE FIRST: Others here on board?

THE FIFTH: I know of one. He doesn't know that I know about him.

THE FIRST: I tremble at what I am about to hear. You speak dangerously.

THE FIFTH: We were leaving port last night. I was on watch and heard a man taking leave of one of our cadets. This is the way it went; the words are chiselled in me as into solid stone: Go then, go then, young fellow. I know you won't come back. Out there is a wave restlessly surging, waiting to bring you your death. A piece of unfeeling metal waits now to bore its way into your breast. You won't come back. Yet a single one of our days together—and they were many—would have been a sun travelling with us through time on a star at our side in the fearful night, and so you will go through life with me until my time is up. You know the duties of a noble body. Calm acceptance of death—if it must be—is the least of them. Die, then, with calm acceptance! Die without illusion! Oh, if the world had seen but one of our days together, it would turn from its error. Die happy! Leave the obsessed! Remember all that has been between us; all that can be between two human creatures. Remember this at the last moment. No Hope or God takes the terror out of death. Just one thing: remembering what was and can be between man and man. And if there should be —which I doubt—new worlds beyond this one, spinning within our reach, then this thought is the leap towards the new goal; what human relationships can be.

THE FIRST: These two spoke like that? Like that?

THE FIFTH: They continued to speak quietly together. I heard the older one give the younger some advice. I heard things of such a familiar ring, things so close to my heart, so bright with light, that I had to run away for fear of forgetting my duty.

THE FIRST: They really spoke that way?

THE FIFTH: I felt these men were already living the life which I had only sensed as possible. And held life worthy of the highest efforts. As if they possessed something even in this world which had raised them above all life and death.

THE FIRST: If you make mankind so full of riches, God will simply die.

THE FIFTH: If the ocean beneath my feet had turned to fire, I couldn't have been more startled than when I heard this. Now I shall fear neither Death nor Disgrace!

THE FIRST: What are you saying: Death and Disgrace?

THE FIFTH: Now I know this, I will fear neither Death nor Disgrace.

THE FIRST: What do you mean? What are you after? What is it?

THE FIFTH: Disgrace and Death are my certain lot.

THE FIRST: Action at sea means death.

THE FIFTH: Oh, how blind you are!

THE FIRST: If we go into action, all will die!

THE FIFTH: I shall die even if we don't.

THE FIRST: Man, man, what are you thinking of? Be warned. Do you know what death is!

THE FIFTH: A word. A thing long since outlived.

THE FIRST: What are you thinking of? For pity's sake, man, what are you thinking of?

THE FIFTH: Of my lot.

THE FIRST: On which path?

THE FIFTH: The one allotted me.

THE FIRST: Can't I take it, too?

THE FIFTH: You take it, too?

THE FIRST: Someone to go along with you? No man likes going alone. But many must.

At this moment, the sleeping Sailors are again audible in their dreams.

THE THIRD: Nothing.

THE SECOND: Wisps of smoke?

THE THIRD: Nothing.

THE SECOND: Wisps of smoke?

THE THIRD: Bow wave, white, far off! Bow wave!

THE SECOND: Eh?

THE THIRD: Nothing.

THE SECOND: Wisps of smoke!

THE THIRD: Ships! Ships!

THE SECOND: Ships! Ships!

THE THIRD: Action! Action!

THE SECOND: Action! Action!

THE THIRD: The long guns swivel.

THE SECOND: Raise muzzles to the sky.

THE THIRD: The war-like pennants fly.

THE SECOND: The dice rise—pause—fall. Fire, steam-clouds! Quiet! Keep your eyes on the sea.

THE THIRD: Long-fingered Death reaches out for the ships. The ships unseeing destroy each other. Are gone.

THE SECOND: Fire, flash, steam-clouds! On! On! They are fattening us for the kill. Faster. Faster. Gulp it down, it's got no taste.

THE THIRD: The hour strikes only once. This is it.

THE FOURTH: Somebody help me wake up. Please, somebody, help me wake up! We're only dreaming, can't you see, we're only dreaming!

THE FIRST: What a racket! What's wrong with you, mate? Where are you now?

THE SECOND: Shrapnel, smoke, fire. The first blow from the beast!

THE THIRD: Means another's coming! Strike! Strike!

THE SECOND: Be dead certain!

THE THIRD: We are what we thought we were.

THE SECOND: Finish them off!

THE THIRD: Finish them! Finish them!

THE SECOND: Finish them! Ha ha ha ha!

THE THIRD: Finish them! Ha ha ha!

They laugh in their dreams.

THE SECOND: Have we finished them off?

THE THIRD: We have.

THE SECOND: Then quiet now!

The men have quietened.

THE FIRST: That was the dream of action.

THE FIFTH: They're a plucky lot!

THE FIRST: How they laughed in their dreams!

THE FIFTH: They're plucky all right!

THE FIRST: How they laughed!

THE FIFTH: All they needed was the right cue Mate, if we do have some action now, what will you do?

THE FIRST: Obey. What else? And you?

THE FIFTH: Give them the right cue!

THE FIRST: There is only one thing for it, obey, conform and go to your doom. Any step whatsoever means the end of us too.

THE FIFTH: You can be disobedient and still obey!

THE FIRST: Madman! You're surely not thinking of . . . !

THE FIFTH: Obey something higher.

THE FIRST: Madman! Madman! Friend, brother, comrade, listen to me, listen to what I'm saying!

THE FIFTH: It's true, isn't it: we all feel it.

THE FIRST: Against the most merciless force, against something all are subject to, and everyone bows down to, no matter what else inspires them, something no-one can revolt against—

THE FIFTH: Sometime it must crumble!

THE FIRST: Not here, man! Not here on this ship sailing into action. In this complex of men and steel, where do you expect to find the weak spot?

THE FIFTH: Have you understood so little of what I said?

THE FIRST: You're committing suicide! You are sinning against yourself!

THE FIFTH: You are committing murder—you are murdering each other, all of you!

THE FIRST: Madman! You rage against yourself alone!

THE FIFTH: Didn't you yourself say—

THE FIRST: I only spoke of it. Didn't consider doing anything.

THE FIFTH: Remember, and be a man.

THE FIRST: What is going to happen? Oh, God Almighty, what is going to happen?

THE FIFTH: Be a man!

THE FIRST: Shrink from the deed!

THE FIFTH: Isn't this my destiny as a man?

THE FIRST: A deed is always a thrust in the dark.

THE FIFTH: It can strike sparks.

THE FIRST: Acting with violence is like a blind man flailing in the dark. My comrade, my friend, listen to me. My life has seen little, but this I know: action is always accursed. Wait for things

95

to mature! Wait and see what will come of itself. By action you always destroy what is great and of value in things.

THE FIFTH: Miserable blubbering!

THE FIRST: Don't try to think out what you will do! Don't try to know what you will be like. Wanting to know is also a kind of weakness. Promise me, mate: wait and see how things turn out. Wait! Wait!

THE FIFTH: If we go into action, good, you'll obey. But I won't. Now you know.

The SECOND, THIRD *and* FOURTH SAILORS *have awakened and hear the following.*

THE FIRST: Oh, if only it doesn't come to that! If only the day were over. If only that were still possible.

THE THIRD: Do you hear? Did you hear him?

THE SECOND: We're quite awake, aren't we?

THE FIFTH: Even if we see no action, I will no longer obey orders.

THE THIRD: There you have it. No shadow of doubt.

THE SECOND: It was said!

THE THIRD: Will we take him now?

THE SECOND: Let's take him!

THE THIRD: Mutiny! Ho! Mutiny! Tie him up.

THE SECOND: Mutiny! Mutiny!

THE FIRST: Who's starting the mutiny?

THE THIRD: You are.

THE SECOND: The two of you!

THE FIRST: Me?

THE FIFTH: Not him. Men, I swear his conscience is clear.

THE SECOND: You, though!

THE THIRD: Didn't you just say you're no longer going to obey orders, didn't you try to get him to go along with you? Who knows what else you were planning.

THE FIFTH: You've known me now for as long as I've known you. Have you suddenly turned into bloodhounds?

THE SECOND: Have you been doing these things?

THE FIFTH: What I was saying concerns me alone. What I'm about to say—pay attention—concerns the rest of you.

THE FIRST: *at the port-hole*] He hasn't done anything yet, and yet

96

it's already upon him. Save him, save him, Heaven! Help us all! What's that? What's that out there? Eyes, oh, my eyes!

THE THIRD: All we're concerned with is whether you confess.

THE FIRST: *at the port-hole*] What's that out there on the horizon? Oh, shipmates! Shipmates!

THE FIFTH: Who's that shouting?

THE SECOND: Are you confessing?

THE FIFTH: I confess. Even more: I'll do what I said I would.

THE FIRST: *at the port-hole*] Shipmates, shipmates! What's that coming up over there? This is goodbye to everything

THE FIFTH: Who's doing all that singing?

THE THIRD: Let's take him before the captain.

THE FOURTH: *who has so far been looking on, now gets up*] Not so fast, not so rash, you blokes!

THE FIRST: *at the port-hole*] Skaggerak! Skaggerak! The last day of May! Victory day! Judgment day! Goodbye to home, country and everything!

THE SECOND: Mutiny, did you hear?

THE THIRD: Mutiny, we heard.

THE FOURTH: I heard, too.

THE SECOND: And you stand there so calmly!

THE THIRD: And you stand there so calmly!

THE FOURTH: Take your hands off him!

THE SECOND: This is the limit.

THE FOURTH: Let him go!

THE SECOND: Are you trying to make fools of us?

THE THIRD: What do you intend to do? That's what I want to know.

THE SECOND: Still nothing? Is that the idea?

THE FOURTH: Let him go!

THE THIRD: What's the world coming to?

THE SECOND: Common-sense gets you nowhere these days.

THE FIRST: *at the port-hole*] It's them! Oh, day of victory. Oh day of lamentation! The last, last day of May, the turning-point, the end! Ships, ships, it's them.

THE FOURTH: Don't put too much faith in what you've been taught, mates. Things are their own teachers. Learn from them. Have we only known him since yesterday? You know what words are! Don't make such a fuss over every jack-sparrow. That

97

D

'taking-things-seriously' business is no good. What a man says may sound fine. When it comes to doing, one man is the same as the next. Quiet, mutineers! In essential things, of course. Don't make so much out of things that don't matter. Don't try to be more particular than Old Man God himself who had all seven days of Creation to worry about. What a hoo-ha! Have you only known the man since yesterday? Haven't you smoked a pipe or two of tobacco with him? And now you pounce on him after a couple of words and it wouldn't take much more before you'd tear him to pieces. All it needs is the sound of the pipe and the drum! Let him feel the sound leap in his blood. Let him listen, prick up his ears, hear the old familiar strain. Bet my boots: he'll do what he's trained to do. Quiet, man. Nobody's getting at you. You've made up your mind too quick, that's your trouble.

THE FIFTH: You'll be the first—

THE FOURTH: Nobody's first. That's all nonsense. As long as you keep worrying about the difference between big and little, rough and smooth, and God knows what, you're nothing but a schoolboy, if you see what I mean.

THE FIRST: *at the port-hole*] Shipmates! Shipmates! This is it! Ships. Ships. They are quite clear now! Come here. Ships. Ships. This is it.

THE SECOND: Christ, what's he shouting about?

THE THIRD: What rubbish is that he's shouting?

THE SECOND: Not seeing things again, man, like the things you saw in the blue sky?

THE THIRD: Ships, does he say he can see? Ships?

THE FOURTH: Yes, there they are boys. Ships: with lines like that they must be warships! Over there! Look! Take a good look! This is it boys!

THE SECOND: This means action!

THE THIRD: Shipmates! Shipmates! Blue-jackets!

THE SECOND: This means action all right!

THE THIRD: What's mine is yours!

THE FOURTH: Your hour has come, men!

THE SECOND: Action it is then. And today!

THE THIRD: Angels, you are angels! What can I buy you. Pretty as roses! Come on, what can I get you!

THE SECOND: We're going mad.

THE THIRD: Action! Action on the high seas! Trial of strength and test who is the better, who's the better seaman!

At this moment pipe and drum sound.

THE SECOND: Listen! Pipe and drum! Listen! Pipe and drum!

THE THIRD: Clear the decks for action. If you're a man at all, your heart must leap.

THE FIFTH: What are they doing? What do I see? What's happening inside them?

Is this the way it starts?

THE FOURTH: They are hugging each other and dancing!

THE FIFTH: Is this how action starts? What is this thing?

THE FOURTH: Take a good look. Don't be an idiot. Take a good look first! There will still be time to do what you have to do. There is always a time and place for madness!

THE FIFTH: Flashes of lightning are scorching me. Lightning. What is action? What's happening? Are we still the men we were?

THE FOURTH: The ultimate is now being revealed, what's behind it all young fellow!

THE SECOND: Come with us, brother! Come! Live!

THE THIRD: Come with us, brother! Come! Win!

THE FOURTH: Just come with us and die, boy!

THE FIFTH: With you! With you? God, lads, you've no idea how different you look! What's getting into me?

THE SECOND: We are, and the battle!

THE THIRD: The battle and all of us!

THE FIFTH: I swear, I swear, the other thing—

THE FOURTH: That'll come, that'll come too!

Pipe and drum sound for the second time.

THE SECOND: Do you hear! Do you hear!

THE FIFTH: What a joyful sound!

THE SECOND: Come on! And live!

THE THIRD: Come on! And win!

THE FOURTH: Come all and die!

THE FIFTH: Battle! Battle! Where will the battle lead us?

Exeunt. For a moment the turret is empty. Then the men return. From now on the words written down are interspersed with orders and shouts of activity during the battle.

THE SECOND: Four against four.

THE THIRD: You ought to see the supporting fleet on both sides.

THE SECOND: Going to be no joke.

THE THIRD: Lads! Lads! Blue-jackets!

THE FOURTH: Quiet. Don't get excited. Everything ship-shape? See everything is working smoothly! No time for flag-waving! No time for shooting off your mouth! No getting impatient! No more to it than a job to be done! No going soft! No bragging or boasting! Let's see the New Man this age has produced.

THE THIRD: Lads, lads, blue-jackets! Samoa was so wonderful!

THE SECOND: Tell us!

THE THIRD: Takes a long time.

THE FOURTH: Sun shining down on it. Let it. Wave upon wave roaring down on the shore there. Let 'em.

THE THIRD: Heat in here would drive you mad!

Bell rings. A shot.

THE SECOND: *observing*] Too far.

Bell rings. A shot.

THE SECOND: *observing*] Too short.

THE THIRD: Third time lucky.

Bell rings. A shot.

THE SECOND: *observing*] A hit. Smoke. Fire! A column shoots up to the clouds. Got him!

THE THIRD: Take a breather, things are rolling.

THE SECOND: If you're going to hit, you'll hit.

THE SIXTH: If you're going to be hit, you'll be hit.

THE SECOND: Practice-firing, lads!

THE THIRD: Practice-firing, that's all it is.

THE FOURTH: Well, any way, if any of you ever gets a spud between his teeth again, say hullo to it from me.

THE SECOND: If any of you ever catches a lady-bird again, give her a kiss from me.

THE THIRD: If any of you ever sees a pretty little elf again, do her for me!

THE SECOND: There are plenty others can do that! And trained up to it, too.

THE THIRD: Took a hard school, though!

THE FIFTH: We must be in the thick of it already. Stop, slow down, not so fast. I can't keep up. Have you nothing to say? Aren't you surprised at me? Boys, I've never felt like this in my life before. Boys, listen a minute. I've got something to tell you.

THE FOURTH: Keep it to yourself!

THE FIFTH: But it's to do with you and me.

THE FOURTH: We know! Keep it to yourself!

THE SECOND: This shooting!

THE THIRD: Our bodies! But we'll get our fill. Not down here, but up here [*points first to his belly, then to his chest*]. Anybody ever worked like this before?

THE SECOND: Pay's good, too.

THE THIRD: All I'm asking is whether anyone's ever worked like this before.

THE SECOND: Tempo! Dance! Dance-tempo . . . Who can I ask for the next dance—strict tempo? [*Laughter*].

THE THIRD: Now you can see what you're capable of!

THE SECOND: No need to father children to show what you can do!

THE THIRD: Shut up about women right now!!

THE SECOND: What about after? What then? Then comes the sweet reward!

THE FIRST: Don't be so blind, lads, and cynical. Any second can carry us off. Then that's the end of us.

THE THIRD: So what?

THE SECOND: Dance-tempo.

THE THIRD: Suppose you mean we still have a bit of time to learn. You're making a big mistake. Either way. Are what we are. Save up your love. We'll have had our fill before then, not here, but here. That's all that matters.

THE FIFTH: Anything to be seen?

THE SECOND: Nothing more. Sun's gone. Smoke and haze over the whole sea.

THE FIFTH: No more shooting from the other side.

THE SECOND: We're not shooting either.

THE THIRD: Pity we're walled up so tight. Know nothing, see nothing until your number's up.

THE SECOND: Same thing anywhere else. But you'll get your fill. Not here, but here.

THE FIFTH: Why the lull in the battle?

THE FOURTH: Who wants to know?

THE FIFTH: I do.

THE FOURTH: Just take a look at this fellow. Warming up to it a bit, eh?

THE THIRD: Suppose we ought to tell him we're sorry now.

THE FIFTH: Sorry? What? Tell who? What for?

THE THIRD: I thought you were a coward earlier on, when you were sitting there mumbling away.

THE SECOND: Well, he was ready to mutiny, the bastard.

THE THIRD: That's different.

THE FIFTH: Why the lull in the battle? Come on, let it roar. In all its splendour and terror. My lungs breathe it in, my every pulse sings battle, battle descend upon us! The seed once sown must grow, even if it shatters us! What is once let loose must roll, even if we are crushed beneath it! What has once begun must be finished! Don't be like lambs to the slaughter! Drive yourselves on like tigers! Keep going to the end. And whoever keeps on to the end—whip on the stars if they refuse to move!

THE SECOND: Gently, mate! Gently! Where do you get all those lovely metaphors and images from?

THE FIRST: My legs are trembling.

THE SECOND: Funk of course!

THE FOURTH: With or without funk: keep going!

THE FIRST: It's all right, it's gone.

Bell rings. A shot.

THE SECOND: *observing*] Smoke everywhere. A miss! Ah! no! Explosion, flames up to the skies! Something's rising! Falling back! Smoke clouds, flames, steam vapour. Hell and damnation, it's quiet there now. Nothing more! Nothing. A ship has just gone down.

ALL: A ship sunk!

THE SIXTH: How fast a ship sinks.

THE SECOND: You hardly get a chance to—

THE SIXTH: Must be a wonderful sight.

THE THIRD: Lads, lads, blue-jackets. Now it's getting under way. We'll get our fill; not here, but here! Bring them to heel. Break their pride. Then we'll pardon them all and be good friends again!

THE SECOND: When they stop ruling the waves, then we'll be friends again.

THE THIRD: We'll get our fill, not here, but here.

THE SECOND: Even if your belly bursts.

THE FIRST: I'm beginning to get the shakes again. It is upon us.

THE THIRD: What's that I hear! What rubbish is he talking?

THE FIRST: It is upon us!

THE SECOND: Why not under us?

THE FOURTH: Quiet! Keep still! No shouting!

THE SECOND: If you're hit, you're hit.

THE FIFTH: It's coming! It's coming! Oh! Oh! Out of here. Let me out. I won't, I won't!

THE FOURTH: That won't do you any good! Hold still, just hold still!

Explosion in the turret. It fills with smoke. All are lying on the floor, only the THIRD SAILOR *stands leaning against the armour-plating, dying.*

THE SECOND: Not bad for a start, eh? That's showing us, eh? But the armour-plating held, eh? Everyone still alive. Right? Thanks a lot, armour-plating, thanks a lot, thanks a lot. Up and man the gun!

THE FIRST: That's the way the blow falls. That's how it falls and you never know where it came from. Whether you're ready or not. We could all have been at the bottom by this time. The lot of us.

THE SECOND: Shut up, man! Get up. And help the others. Up, all hands, show a leg! We've always come through all right, and always will! Take care you don't swallow too much of it. It'll make you dizzy and fog your head! If you're going to hit, you'll hit; if you're hit, you're hit.

THE THIRD: *dying*] Oil, oil, sweet oil for my head. Come on, give me dogdaisies and oil. Play, music! Chords, full chords; soft, sweet, full chords, give them to me! Oil, oil, sweet oil for my head. Put on all your blue colours and put on your pretty coloured caps. And play, play, play on! Dance, dance on! Oil, oil, sweet oil for my head! Blindfold my eyes! Blindfolds, blindfolds! Friends, I will lead the dance.

He collapses and dies.

THE SECOND: Cut it out, man. What? Has he been hit? Have you been hit, lad? Come on, joker! Mate! Say no, no, no! It's just a joke! Yes, yes, yes! Get up! To the gun. There's still a lot to do. Think he's going to die? It certainly looks as though he is! He's already dead, is he? Samoa! Hey, Samoa! Shout, yell: Samoa! Hell, that doesn't take long! Almost no time at all! Samoa. Samoa. Dead's dead.

The others all get up again gradually.

THE FOURTH: Don't start thinking! Back to the gun!
THE SECOND: What great mates this corpse and me were. Till just a minute ago. Mustn't start thinking about it; that's right.
THE SIXTH: Sure he's quite dead?
THE SECOND: Dead. Horribly dead. Leave him.
THE FIFTH: Boys, is it true that I swore at you earlier on?
THE SECOND: Not that I noticed.
THE FIFTH: I like action. It will cost us our lives in a minute. But before that our lungs heave, hearts race, muscles jump. All that damned questioning, lads, where's it gone?
THE SECOND: Getting on your high horse again, are you?
THE FIFTH: I take over the dead man's place!
THE FIRST: Outside or inside, it makes all the difference.

Shrapnel against turret.

THE SECOND: Ha ha ha, the turret holds. Do you hear the hailstorm outside. The good old turret will hold!

The door is flung open, a voice calls.

VOICE: Any dead?
THE FOURTH: One.
VOICE: Any wounded?
THE FOURTH: None.
VOICE: Hand your dead man out. [*They hand out* THIRD SAILOR *quickly*]. Everything ship-shape otherwise?
THE FOURTH: Everything ship-shape.
VOICE: We have sunk one ship and damaged another. Hit four times ourselves. The action continues. Keep it up!

The door is shut.

THE SIXTH: The action continues.
THE FIRST: Oil, oil, sweet oil for my head, that's what he said.
THE FOURTH: The action continues!
THE SECOND: No more of your questioning here, man! Keep your questions for the other side, in that Beyond of yours.

The door opens again, a man enters.

THE SEVENTH: Replacement reporting.
THE SECOND: Are things the same in the other turrets, you Yid?
THE SEVENTH: Same everywhere, you Christian! In the third turret, they're singing and praying so loudly, you can hear it from outside. They say that a couple in the first have started dancing. You want to watch out for fumes!
THE SECOND: Pretty much like pigs, we are. Lining up to be butchered.
THE FIFTH: Doesn't matter. Now one man can recognize another again, now something grows among men that more than makes up for all suffering. Isn't the sweat of it strong in you? Blood! Blood! The only thing that brings out the truth.
THE FIRST: No, listen to me, men! Take thought. Try to act like human beings!
THE SECOND: Aren't we human as we are, then? Aren't we maybe heroes into the bargain?
THE FOURTH: It's just our age was born to blood, that's all! Hero or coward—where's the difference? We're running down—clocks with hands gone mad! Stand still, stand still. Till the clockwork runs down.

D*

THE SECOND: But why here in the turret?
THE FOURTH: Because you must!
THE SECOND: Why must I?
THE FOURTH: Because you can't do otherwise.
THE SECOND: Why can't I do otherwise?
THE FOURTH: Because you're an ass.
THE SECOND: A pig would be better, a pig waiting for the butcher.
THE FIRST: There it is again!

Explosion. They fall down.

THE FOURTH: The action continues.
THE SECOND: That hurts.
THE FIFTH: Hell, that really flattens you.
THE SEVENTH: It'll be the same for them on the other side.
THE FOURTH: Not bad shots, either.
THE SEVENTH: They'll be men much the same as us. Not a bit better or worse!
THE FOURTH: No philosophising. Back to the gun!
THE SECOND: *singing*] Soft and gentle, she is smiling, how she's smiling, can't you see?
THE FIFTH: Who's smiling, mate?
THE SECOND: That nit there!

Continues singing.

THE SIXTH: Away from my nose, dog! Down, boy, get away from my nose.
THE FIFTH: Who's at your nose, mate?
THE SIXTH: A dog.
THE FOURTH: Pull yourselves together, boys. A seaman swims like a lump of lead, land is cheap on the ocean-bed. Don't you think that's funny?
THE SECOND: Why laugh? Why cry?
THE FOURTH: Keep cool now! Just get on with the job. Pull yourselves together. Don't let these foul fumes get the better of you. Keep on top! Somebody put my hand out, would you? It's on fire.
THE FIFTH: Are we hearing right? What did you say? I hope to God I heard wrong. Is your hand on fire?

THE FOURTH: Put it out, put it out, you bastards! Can't you see my hand burning?

THE SEVENTH: Madness setting in.

THE FIFTH: Catch him by the throat straight away! Man, you'll have to get away from the gun. With force if not willingly. Grab him.

THE FOURTH: Put it out! Put it out! I'll have the lot of you strung up, you bastards. This one's a mutineer. That one's had it coming for a long time. Hang him! Hang him! That's an order!

THE FIFTH: You're not giving the orders any more, mate. Listen to me, men. Get that madman away from the gun.

THE FOURTH: Don't be angry, matey. Come and make up again! We are the only two still in our right minds. We can do it. And if there's no more we can do, there's no more we can do. Then it doesn't matter, eh?

THE FIRST: How soon you forget. He's back on the gun already, quite happy. We know, don't we, men: what we are doing means something else entirely. Is this an armoured turret and nothing more, that's what I want to ask?

THE FOURTH: What more would it be than an armoured turret?

THE FIRST: A bell, maybe? A bell along with all the other bells? Ding-dong, ding-dong—that's how they ring.

THE FOURTH: Tell me, what's really happening in this turret? Tell me! Can't they let us drown in peace? Is: 'madness, mistake' to be shouted across our honourable graves? Can't they let us find a quiet resting-place in the water? Damn the man who disturbs our bones. Words, oh words: damned fiddling about!

THE FIFTH: Be quiet, boy, that's just somebody babbling on like his grandfather did. If you want a bit of sport, ask him about the higher powers and get him to bless you!

THE FIRST: What can be between man and man: ask him about that!

THE FIFTH: The action continues.

Bell rings. Shot.

THE FOURTH: Hear, hear! Bless him! Bless him three times over, whoever's doing the shooting!

Bell rings. Shot.

THE FOURTH: Shoot! Shoot! Shoot! Do nothing else but: shoot!

Door opens and gas-masks are thrown in.

VOICE: Masks!

Door shuts again.

THE FIFTH: Masks on!

Men obey and from now on it is impossible to tell one from the other.
FIFTH SAILOR *stands at the gun alone. Bell rings. Shot.*

THE FOURTH: Hear, hear, lads! Bless him three times over, whoever's
doing the shooting. Beg him, beseech him to keep on shooting.
Down on your knees before him! When everything gets out of
hand, when madness rules, when all we can do is twitch, when
we can no longer keep silent and the flesh screams and screams,
then shoot, boy! Go on shooting, shoot! Shoot on regardless!
Shoot!

THE SECOND: Save our lives!

ALL: Our lives, our lives, save them. Stay alive, alive, alive.

*Explosion. The light is completely extinguished. The men are all
on the floor, indistinguishable, because of their gas-masks. One is
still standing at the gun, clutching his gas-mask on.*

MAN AT THE GUN: The action continues.

VOICES: A drink! A drink! Water! Put it out! What happened?
Where are we? Everything is turning against us! Water! Give
us water! Light!

MAN AT THE GUN: Praise be for the battle, boys, praise be. We'll
carry on in the dark. What do you want light for? All just
imagination. Up, boys, up! Who still has a muscle left? Who
still has a heart-beat to spare? Things are just getting under way
now. Aren't you enjoying it? You've got to be in to win!
Don't coddle yourselves so much. The seed once sown must
grow, even if it shatters us. What is once let loose must roll
even if it crushes us. Come on, my lads, come on to the end. Whoever, sticks it out to the end—well, I can't promise eternal bliss,
but it's got to be done.

VOICES: Up, lads, up. If you've still a muscle left. Up, lads, up, if you've still a heart-beat to spare. Things are just getting under way.

MAN AT THE GUN: The action continues.

VOICE: A seer. A man who sees in the dark! A man who sees signs in the blue sky! Signs, signs, give us a sign! What's to come? Where are we heading for? Where are we going? Will we survive?

ALL: Will we survive? Will we survive?

The light goes on again. The man at the gun can now be clearly seen and the others stretched out, but trying to get up. The SIXTH SAILOR *is just dying.*

VOICE: *to the* SIXTH] What are you trying to say? Why are you moving your lips? Speak, tell me. I can't help you.

SIXTH: Dogs! Dogs!

VOICE: Don't blame us. You're not being fair to us.

The SIXTH SAILOR *dies.*

VOICES: Hear the rushing. Rushing? Hear the droning. Droning? Feel the shuddering, Shuddering? Feel the rocking. Rocking? What's happening? What are they doing to us? What's going on? We want to live! Live! Live!

VOICE: On your knees! On your knees! [*The men go down on their knees, raise their hands in supplication and slither along behind the speaker*]. The world rests in your wisdom. Time flows from your will. Life struggles towards your heart. We must go as you direct. We are but snow-flakes that fall in your storm. Bullets that fly, hurled by your hand. Sparks blown over the waters. See, we know this. How should our will strive against yours? How should we plan to thwart your wisdom, how preserve life split from your heart? See, see, we did not choose the way, we had no power over the hands we raised. Yes, yes, we did do it, did act, did raise our hands. Ours is the guilt.

VOICES: Do you hear, do you hear talk of guilt? Who speaks like this? Strike him dead. Shut his mouth. No guilt, no guilt! We did it and would do it again. We want to live! Live!

VOICE: Sainted asses, that's all you are! Machines running down, clocks with hands running wild. Keep calm. Don't make a noise, drown, can't you. Die, won't you. Let others die in peace!

VOICE: We've been long on our knees. [*Explosion. Complete chaos*]. Fatherland, Fatherland, my dear Fatherland. We are pigs, waiting for the butcher. We are calves, waiting for the knife. Our blood will stain the fish red! Fatherland, see, see, see! Pigs to the slaughter, calves to the knife! Whole flocks, smashed by the lightning. The blow, the blow, when will it fall? Fatherland, Fatherland, what more do you have in store for us?

VOICES: Fatherland, Fatherland, what more is in store! Fatherland, Fatherland, death devours us like grains of rice. See us prostrate here, Fatherland. Give us death! Death! Death! Give us death, death!

Explosion. The FIRST, FOURTH *and* FIFTH SAILORS *lie with their gas-masks torn off, dying on the floor.*

THE FIRST: Captain! Captain! Is everything all right now? Are we dead?

THE FIFTH: The action continues!

THE FOURTH: We are not dead yet. No need for unseemly haste. We are not dead yet.

THE FIFTH: The action continues!

THE FIRST: Oh, but everything is going to be all right now, isn't it? I'm dying. Now shall I see?

THE FOURTH: 'Course you won't see anything!

THE FIFTH: Can't you hear? Is it quiet? Is the battle won?

THE FOURTH: You'll never know that, either.

THE FIFTH: Hey, you there! Open your eyes!

THE FOURTH: Is that you, mutineer? It's quiet.

THE FIFTH: No, listen, the action continues.

THE FOURTH: Tell me! But what for?—It's all the same from first to last. Ask anyway: Why did you not mutiny?

THE FIFTH: The action continues, do you hear? Don't close your eyes yet. I make a good gunner, eh? I'd have made a good mutineer, too! But firing a gun came easier? Eh? Must just have come easier?

END

ANTIGONE

TRAGEDY IN FIVE ACTS

by

Walter Hasenclever

1917

Dedicated to Tilla Durieux

Translated by J. M. Ritchie

ANTIGONE

Characters

PEOPLE OF THEBES

CREON, *King of Thebes*

EURYDICE, *his Queen*

HAEMON, *his Son*

ANTIGONE

ISMENE

TIRESIAS

GUARDS

CAPTAIN

HERALD

Scene: the city and the palace of Thebes.
The palace in the background.
In the centre the castle gateway opens on to a platform.
This is the theatre of the king.
Steps lead down into the arena.
Three entrances: right, left and opposite the palace.
This is the theatre of the people.

ACT I

The stage is dark.
Fanfares. Palace and arena become light. People streaming into the arena. The gate of the palace opens. The HERALD *steps out.*

Scene 1

HERALD. PEOPLE.

Herald: The war is over. Our enemies are defeated.
The city is free.
Eteocles, the king, fell
In single combat with his brother Polynices;
Both died horribly by the sword.
Eteocles is dead. Creon is king.
Creon decrees:

That the bodies of the fallen be buried;
Bonfires lit and thanksgiving made
To the Gods for saving our homeland.
Let Eteocles be given a burial,
A royal burial,
Worthy of his ashes: hero and saviour.
But Polynices, the traitor, poisonous scion
From the shades of Oedipus, who marched
With the company of Seven against Thebes,
To seize power for himself—remains where he lies
On the battle-field, spoil for dogs and crows.
His foul carrion stinks to heaven,
Monument to all men of his disgrace.
Creon commands:
Whosoever violates
This dread decree—
Whosoever pays last respects to this body
Shall be stoned to death,
His corpse shall join the other.
Thus we avenge the deeds of our enemies!

Exit. Trumpets.

A Citizen: Many have fallen in the war.
2nd Citizen: Times are hard.
3rd Citizen: Why should we not bury Polynices?
Many Voices: The war was his fault.—He wanted to kill the king.
              He is a dog, let him be eaten by the dogs.
A Warrior: He was a warrior like us. He was brave.
2nd Warrior: He was the enemy.
A Woman: Perhaps he has a wife and children.
Many Women: We too have children—who helps us?
1st Citizen: We have a good king.
2nd Citizen: A brave king. He's on the throne!

Laughter.

1st Warrior: *threateningly*] Creon is king!
1st Citizen: The brother-in-law of Oedipus.
2nd Citizen: *sotto voce*] The curse of Oedipus . . .

1st Warrior: Obey the king!
2nd Warrior: He gives us wine.
Voices: Wine!—When warriors return.—
        Wine in abundance!—Flutes and dancing-girls.
3rd Citizen: First let us bury the dead.

Silence.

A Woman: What about the widows and orphans?
2nd Woman: Our men are dead. We are hungry. Give us food!
1st Citizen: We want no more war.
Many Voices: We want peace!
A Youth: *standing on the steps*] Listen to me. We are young.
        New generations of men are born.
        We shall march. War is glorious.
1st Citizen: Green Youth!
2nd Youth: *alongside the first*] When the battle rends us,
        You shall not feel it,
        You shall not starve.
Many Shouts: Thebes! Thebes!

Music of flutes off stage.

3rd Youth: *alongside the other two*] The world is wide.
        We shall conquer many enemies.
        Forward, friends—immortality!
Many Women: How they shout!

They press forward to them.

1st Warrior *to a girl*] Come closer, my little joy!

He takes her in his arms.

The Girl: A gloomy crowd, these citizens!
2nd Warrior: This night wine,
        The strangler of worry, flows.
The Girl: This night, this night—
1st Warrior: Hotter than battle—
2nd Warrior: All must drink their fill!

The Youths:	Victory is ours. Life is ours. Seven armies before seven gates in Thebes! Tell the peoples of the earth to come— We are armed. Who will dare attack us?
Several:	*noisily*] We are armed. Who will dare attack us?
Many:	The fatherland is saved.
All:	Long live the king!
1st Citizen:	Go home to your houses. The day is at an end.
2nd Citizen:	Two women approach—there . . .

All turn round.

1st Citizen:	Quiet. The princesses: Antigone and Ismene. The sisters of the dead men. Honour their sorrow. Let us go.

All off.

Scene 2

ANTIGONE *and* ISMENE *enter right. The palace is dark. The arena is light.*

Antigone:	Come to the steps, where as children We played before the house of Oedipus. Ismene, here— He fell, our father— Blinded: father-murderer, mother-ravisher. For the second time the place fills my heart; The crime gnaws at me.

She seats herself on the steps.

	Our brothers are dead. They call it war. Why must *I* go on living on their graves?
Ismene:	You will not die. Light the flame of hope! Behold, peace returns. I will comfort you. Weep, dear sister!
Antigone:	*plunges her hands into the earth*] I claw my way into the earth. It is not so unyielding as the hearts of the mighty.

Yonder lies the body of our brother,
Slaughtered like an animal.
Where is it written, sister,
That one may not bury the dead?
He is a man. He is my brother.
I know of no enemies thus debased,
Nor any hatred, that defiles death.

Ismene: God will avenge him.

Antigone: Speak not of God!
Did God give permission for men to murder?
Did God, when presumptious Creon
Trampled underfoot the piteous corpse
Send forth fires and earthquakes,
To stop the mouth of the mocker?
God was silent.

Ismene: Then let us flee.

Antigone: Flee, sister?
Darkness came upon Oedipus.
His guilt was not, that unrecognised
The son slew the father—it was that man
In hatred slew his enemy—man.
When I led the old man by the hand
From the palace into poverty,
Into the gray and distant time,
I knew God's curse upon us!
If all men were blind,
Blows would rain ineffective in space.
They would have to love each other, being helpless.
Here there is still fresh blood. Here let us do penance.

Ismene: Are we not poor?

Antigone: Are we not sisters?
Help me bury Polynices.

Ismene: Antigone—
The penalty is death!

Antigone: Why so hesitant?
Is not our brother more to you than death?

Ismene: You go against the command of the king!

Antigone: Should I make his injustice even greater?

Ismene: Let it be forgotten.

Antigone:	Has Creon forgotten him?
	Is hate alone everlasting? How greatly
	Love has changed among men
	If it yields in the face of death. Why do we talk!
	I want to bury him—not weep over him.
Ismene:	You hate Creon, daughter of Oedipus!
Antigone:	While I live, justice lives.
Ismene:	You are a woman. Obey!
Antigone:	On the day of judgment he will meet me
	And call my spirit to account.
Ismene:	Bow your great head!
	New injustice does not bring down the old;
	You keep alive the endless heartache all to no avail.
	Does not the eye of the citizen
	Awake with laughter towards the bright sun?
	Share the stirrings of common humanity!

Distant music, gradually growing louder till the end of the scene.

Antigone:	Be silent!
	Join the dance to your sensual pleasure.
	Take yourself to safety.
Ismene:	Antigone!
	Go, bare your bosom—
	Since constancy has fled it for the people.
	You are a woman—throw yourself to the men!
Ismene:	The world is more to me than one man,
	Though he were a thousand times my brother.
Antigone:	Go to that world. He never was your brother.
Ismene:	How lonely we are—
Antigone:	Go! Disown me.

Exit right.

Ismene:	*swept away by the crowd that surges in*].

Scene 3

Torches, music. Warrior youths lying around in the centre. Dancing girls are performing a pantomime. They approach, fall back, scatter twigs, allow the youths to seize them and sink down among them. One beautiful girl is left standing with a wreath. She bends down and places it on the brow of the most handsome of the youths.

Dancing Girl: High on the hilltops fires are flaming,
     Fame and glory, prowess far—
     Love us! expend us!—we are yours for the taking,
     Sweet fruit of the vibrant hour.

A Voice: *cuttingly*] What of the dead?

All look round in annoyance.

2nd Voice: Silence there!
A Youth: Who disturbs the feast?
A Citizen: The malcontents!
The Youth Steeds sunk muddy,
with the   Cut throat,
Wreath: Broken body,
    We horsemen went
    Steady
    Through the enemy midst we went.
    In the sky the scarlet scream
    On the ground the bloody stream
    We horsemen went!
    With lance we did tether
    Men like goats together
    Who would not or could not
    Was spitted—on the spot.

He makes the stabbing gesture. Applause.

    How they ran: like hound and hare!
    Old men we left strung up,
    Young men we smashed to pulp.
    Not a life did we spare!
    The crows
    Shall have our foes.

Joyful laughter.

A Voice: The crows?

A Youth: *threateningly*] What was that?

The Voice: Friend! Once upon a time there was a Battle of the Crows. When all the crows were dead, men came and ate them.

The Youth: Jester!

The Voice: The men chose a king, whom they named King of the Crows in memory of the Battle of the Crows. Every ten years they go on a crow hunt. When the crows are killed they prepare a meal for the king. When the king has eaten the crows it takes him ten years to digest them; then the story starts from the beginning again.

A Citizen: A fine tale. Where do all the crows come from?

The Voice: You must ask the king; he knows.

Many Voices: Let Creon come!—The new king.—We want to see the new-crowned king!

The People: Creon!

All turn towards the palace. The palace becomes light. CREON *steps out. Silence.*

Creon: Subjects!
My eyes roam over many lands,
I see cities built, ruling sovereigns;
The palace of kings, eternal marble
On the confused mass of the people.
God, who defeated our enemies, has
Raised me up as king. Heralds have
Proclaimed my will.
I see at my feet good men and bad,
The people of Oedipus, who died long since.
From among you one of his sons arose
As an enemy, to betray his fatherland.
He lies dead and cold now, in his murderous blood
And dreams no more of the throne.
Yet once more I
Here decree with all the might that is mine
No burial place for his body!
May the foul stench of his name

	Make its way into the world where people dwell.
	Woe betide any who associate with his crime.
	All of you must answer equally for his body.
Captain:	We give thanks, King Creon, for avenging us.
	The Guards already stand by the body.
	No-one draws near the outcast now.
Creon:	My people!

Creon: My people!
           The war is won. Mourn your dead.
           Gird yourself for fresh deeds.
           We are surrounded by enemies.
           Only the strong will conquer the world.
           Filled with the spirit of your kings,
           I take power into my hands;
           Honour to friends! Destruction to foes.
           On this day of rejoicing, which you celebrate,
           My bounty too shall be manifest.
           If there is one among you who desires it
           Let him step forward and demand it now.

*The hosts of Poor in grey rags fling themselves down
before the steps. One of them speaks.*

Poor Man: Lord! The fields are not tilled. The cattle are without
            shelter. Our sons were killed in the war.
2nd Poor Man: We die of cold. Our house is sold over our heads.
            Have pity, Lord!
3rd Poor Man: The children die of starvation. The women die of
            fever. Release us from payment of the tribute!
All the Poor: Release us from payment of the tribute!
Creon: I need your money and your sons.
            Thebes shall be mighty once more!
Shouts: Long live Thebes!
The Poor: We are poor.—We want peace.
Creon: See they are given bread.
A Woman: Give us our menfolk!
A Voice: *shrilly*] Down with the rich!
Creon: Who calls there? Come! I want to see you, friend.
            Come closer! What did you say?

A slightly-built boy steps slowly forward.

The Boy:	We are hungry. Yet we must work. Work for the rich. They give us nothing.
Many Voices:	He's right.—Hear him.
Captain:	Silence!
Creon:	*scornfully*] I love this merry lad. What may the world look like Inside his skull?
The Boy:	*suddenly wild, threatening with his fist*] Suffering! Misery!!
Creon:	*darkly*] Why are you screaming, wretch!
The Boy:	*tears open his clothing, stretches out his arms*] I have not eaten for five days. Victories do not fill the belly.
Creon:	Smash him down! Whip him!

Armed men fall upon him and strike him down. He screams. He is dragged away.—Night falls.—Servants with torches stand on the platform.

Take care!
The order of this city is immutable.
Inviolable its ancient law.
Here I stand for all to see:
God gave me majesty,
That I might be a worthy leader.
He alone can call me to account!
I demand obedience in his name.
I shall be good to the good;
Whosoever opposes me I shall crush beneath my foot.

Vague stirring.

Thebes is free. Let the lowest man among you
Live and die for its freedom.
Lay down your weapons and become citizens.
The day will soon dawn, when you can be heroes
once more.
Then I shall call you—the clarion call will sound
Into the roaring cities' furthest dwelling.
To even greater deeds I shall lead you.
Let us add still more to our ancient glory.

They thrust their weapons towards him and beat their shields.

Let wine flow free!
My reign opens with a victory celebration.
The People: Long live Creon!

Scene 4

Through the centre entrance the GUARD *comes in. All recoil from him. He passes along the lane thus formed for him.*

Guard: My Lord . . .
Creon: Who are you?
Guard: A guard from the place of Polynices.
Creon: Speak!
Guard: I dare not, Lord.
Creon: What has happened?
Guard: Lord, a terrible thing!
Creon: Speak!
Guard: *flings himself down*] Do not kill me!
Creon: On your feet, or away with you!
Guard: *gets up slowly*] Polynices—has been—buried!
Creon: Who did this! Where is the one who did it?
Guard: No-one knows. It happened at dusk. A thin layer of dust covers the body, pitted as if with tears. No beast crept up, no tracks of a dog; it must have been someone rising stealthily out of the ground.
Creon: Who was on watch?
Guard: Three men by the fire. We became tired. Some nameless oppression between heaven and earth pressed down upon us. When we awoke, we quarrelled among ourselves. Polynices was buried. No-one dared tell you. We drew lots. I lost. Be merciful!
Creon: Where is the one who did this?
         Up, you warriors! Loose the hounds!
         Fetch him here—alive or dead.

123

The warriors scatter in all directions.

	Am I king?
	Who meddles with impunity in my decrees?
	Am I to believe that God cared
	For the ludicrous thing that lay dead on the ground?
Guard:	Banish me from your sight. Do not ask me to deny a miracle.
Creon:	I spit my scorn on your miracle!
	Will you confess, cur!
Guard:	I did not do it. I am innocent.
Creon:	Away with you! Lick the dust
	Off the corpse with your tongue!

He staggers out. The People murmur disapproval.

An Old Man: King Creon!

Creon: Who speaks unasked?

The Old Man: I am a citizen. I have served many kings. This man is no criminal.

Creon: The spirit of revolt grows in the people.
I see it. I warn you.

The Old Man: I am an old man. Commit no injustice!

Creon: Save your wisdom for others.
Shall wrong triumph?

The Old Man: What is right, what is wrong?

Creon: The rule of law. And I lay down the law!

Darkness.

ACT II

Loud shouts can be heard backstage in all directions. Palace and arena become light. The warriors surge in with weapons upraised. The gate on the platform opens. CREON *steps out.*

Scene 1

CREON. CAPTAIN. PEOPLE.

Captain: Lord!
            We came to the place where the corpse is,
            Alive with teeming vermin.
            Suddenly a storm blows up.
            The earth grows dark,
            Against the horizon stands a maiden
            By the uncovered carrion;
            We seize her and . . .

Scene 2

Antigone: Be silent. I am here.
Creon: Antigone!

They stare at each other.

Antigone: I am your prisoner. Now pass judgment.
Creon: *after a pause*] You know the law?
Antigone: Does one word weigh
            So much by the false standards of this time
            That the dead turn in their graves
            And ask: Who judges their guilt?
Creon: He who survives must be judge.
Antigone: But not over the dead!
Creon: We know who you are.

Antigone: Say: Oedipus.
Voices: *in an undertone*] Oedipus! Oedipus!
Antigone: Was it not here that with rough fists you thrust
                The poor blind man into the night?
                Has God forgiven you so soon? Are you now king?
                Does your reign open with a victory celebration?
Voices: *louder*] Enemy—traitress!
Antigone: Long live this king!
                For all noble men are in the realm of the dead.
                What more is there for you but to stalk through the
                    graves?
                You have conquered. Kill me!
Creon: Not yet.
                No innocent is put to death before my throne.
                Stand here, Antigone, and speak
                Before all the people.
Antigone: What should I say?
                The mob acclaims you great:
                I am too small.
Creon: Do you repent your crime?
Antigone: Crime, Creon?
Creon: Deed then?
Antigone: And if I did repent?
Creon: The law
                Has decreed your death.
Antigone: But hold—
                Where is the spirit behind this law?
                I know a law as yet unwritten,
                Proclaimed to the world by no herald,
                As old as you and I:
                It is called Love.
Creon: By this I recognise the race of Oedipus!
Antigone: Yes, Oedipus was poor and blind,
                But his eyes burned through to the good.
                The blood from his eyes dropped down
                Upon an earth of murderous lust,
                War and deceit, hatred and vanity.
                This beggar starved to death by malice, vengeance
                Of the invisible mob—

Is not he our king?

Uproar. They surge at her.

Antigone: *climbs up the steps, stretches out her hands]*
Hear me!
His body is dead. He lies in his grave
And awaits his dead son.
He will never be king now. Creon is king!

They draw back. She turns towards CREON.

Creon: And never will he see his son's body.
Antigone: But through the blind man my eyes were opened
The light of his eternal goodness shines within me.
Crucify me against your gates,
Dismember me, cremate the pieces.
I shall arise again in the spittle of your mouth
And go again and bury him.
Creon: Hang a cloak over the truth,
Falsehood grins through the holes.
I shall stamp out your arrogance!
Antigone: Defiler of the Dead, you have broken
All human obligations, last restraints,
Universal law.
The cup is full. I do not fear you.
What more is there to fear?
Creon: Power.
Feel it for your crime!
Antigone: O curse, continue,
Sow the seeds of war for unborn ages.
Rejoice, feast your eyes on death agony,
Multiple murderer! God is still in His heaven.
Voices: She blasphemes.—Hear how she blasphemes!
Creon: God is with us. How can a whore speak his name?
Antigone: God is also with the enemy—

Uproar drowns her words.

Shouts: Kill her!
Antigone: People, you shout and stare.

	What price fame and glory?
	Because One has enough, must all starve?
	Because One lives, must all lick the dust?
Creon:	She casts her nets wide.
	Patience. I hear her. Here speaks the last
	Of the race of Oedipus.
Antigone:	I shall not die!
	The faith behind my deeds lives after me.
	You, me and all who are still enemies.
Creon:	For the second time after her brother
	She has betrayed the city.
Shouts:	Strike her down!
Creon:	Does not shame mount to your cheeks,
	Antigone, before this assembled people?
Antigone:	Yours is the fame. So rule, Creon!
	Into your rejoicing
	Will creep the ghost from the grave.
	Think of me!
Creon:	Eteocles died for the honour of his land.
Antigone:	Both wished to rule, both died.
Creon:	Must I be hero and hangman alike?
Antigone:	Honour the dead! One day you too will die.
Creon:	He was the enemy.
Antigone:	All men are brothers.
Creon:	No!
	Crime demands punishment.
Antigone:	Repay wrong with good!
Creon:	I should be a dog fit for a kennel,
	If I as king on the pillar of the throne
	Were to crown wrong with compassion.
	More befitting a slut. Not me.
	Judgment has been passed. He stays where he is.—
	Double wrong has been committed.
	I wash my hands of this blood.
	Speak, my people, what should be done with her.
Many Shouts:	She must die.
One Voice:	She is a princess.
The People:	Stone her!
Creon:	That is the voice of the people!

Ismene:	*runs through the crowd to the steps*] Sister!
	To the people] Cast your stones—
	She is innocent! I did it.
Creon:	Serpent!
Ismene:	The guilt is mine!
Creon:	Answer:
	Did you commit the crime?
Ismene:	Yes.
Antigone:	Too late.
Ismene:	Do not listen to her!
Creon:	Set the trap, it will catch you both!
Ismene:	Now in your need I am by your side.
Antigone:	I need no help.
	Do you not see all those who stand by me?
Ismene:	I see only a mob raging round you.
Antigone:	You are wrong. Brothers and sisters, hear me.
Ismene:	Shall I too throw stones?
	Antigone—
	Give me your hands, as we are women.
Antigone:	Your place is not here.
Ismene:	Let me stay with you.
Antigone:	Go, save yourself.
Ismene:	You thrust me from you?
Antigone:	My fate is not yet fulfilled.
	You live. I must go to my death.
Ismene:	*to* CREON] Lord, alter this destiny.
	You who are king: help her in her need—

CREON *unmoved*.

Ismene:	Are you prepared to slaughter your own son's betrothed?
Creon:	Rather the lowliest slave in my household
	Than a slut for him.
Ismene:	Tyrant!
	You tear her from the arms of your son?
Creon:	The wedding will be in the grave.
Ismene:	*screams*] Have mercy!

E

Creon: *to the people*] All ye, hear the end of this wrongdoer:
            Out there is a vaulted tomb.
            Shut her in that sepulchre
            With the corpse that was her brother.
            There she may bury him for the second time.
            Let her starve to death. Beg for her life.
            This I swear, an oath I shall keep:
            Who does wrong, shall suffer wrong,
            Till obedience atones for the crime.

            He turns away. The gate of the palace opens and closes
            behind him. The light on the platform goes out.

Scene 4

Stirring in the crowd. They press forward to see the sisters.

A Girl: *curiously*] That's what the daughters of Oedipus look
              like.
A Woman: Those soft little hands must deal with the dead.
2nd Woman: Would you rather bake bread?
3rd Woman: Or empty pots, beat carpets. Slip under the sheets
              with slaves.
1st Girl: That is better than wearing pearls.
2nd Girl: That is nicer than burying princes.
3rd Girl: Now you must serve us.
A Citizen: How proud they are, the poppets.
2nd Citizen: They are to blame for the war!
3rd Citizen: They are in league with the enemy.
4th Citizen: They said: there is no enemy!

Indignation.

Ismene: *screams out*] They are going to kill us!
A Warrior: Rip off their veils!
2nd Warrior: Let's see them naked.
3rd Warrior: Let them dance before they die.
Captain: Did you hear? You're to dance naked before the
              people! Unveil!

ISMENE *and* ANTIGONE *stand clinging to each other on the steps.*

Captain:	Come on, you pair of sluts!
A Voice:	Beat them to death!
A Warrior:	We'll share out their flesh.

Two men leap forward and approach them.

A Youth: *rushes between them with drawn dagger]* Back!
Cowardly dogs, back!!
I'll plunge this into any man
Who dares to touch them!

They draw back in amazement. The group of young men stands protectively in front of the women.

The Youth: Princesses! Your beauty is high
Above all ages.
As long as we live
No shame shall reach you.
A Voice: We want no princesses.
2nd Voice: They abuse their fatherland.
3rd Voice: Why do they betray us?
Many Voices: Answer!

Antigone: *takes one step forward. She stands in the semi-circle of youths]*

Citizens of Thebes!
Woe on him who doubts the hearts of men,
When they are creatures deep in misfortune.
If you knew how I weep for you!
To comfort, to help,
I would enfold you in these arms
Which have cradled all pain and suffering.
The fires flare no more on the hill tops.
Victory is extinguished. Together with you
The enemies' heads thud against the bier of
   unfathomed death.
Each one of you I know has a dear one

In the sere of the November fields.
His mouth, his voice from the mouldering pit
Carries this hour's lost sound over.
All those who have departed this world
Cry Love! and again Love! to your hearts!

A Voice: Unveil! Let your long hair lash your breast.

Antigone: *bares breast and head*] I shroud myself in the sorrow
of God's being.
My hair, ashes, fall on my body
By the grave of mankind.

A Woman: Give us food!

Antigone: Woman! You will bear a child.
When will the sword strike its innocent head?
When is the hour of hostility and death?
For what new war will you give it suck?

Stir.

Blond maiden, you will choose a husband.
He will open the arms of your slumber.
The clarion call sounds through the streets.
Blood burns on the ramparts: battle!

Wonderment.

All you who say: War, Enemy, Honour—
Hear your heart, buried in the dust
Of plundered houses, ravaged temples.
Your heart is the enemy. We are all to blame!

Emotion.

Citizens, before you trample me underfoot,
As your king, and master, rightly commands,
I will not try to talk you over—
I am guiltier than any in Thebes.
I shall accept my punishment. Forgive me in death!

Applause.

Lowliest of maids, I accuse myself of this:
I lived and knew: we are killing each other;

And no voice from God's heaven
Roused me to be a saviour.
I accuse myself, that no festering wounds
Ever poisoned my soft pillows;
That I lived lightly on garlands of blossom
While yet one man went hungry.
I accuse myself—I have enjoyed good
But not worked for the good, or men would not be
    enemies.
Only the love that springs from great suffering
Stays the tears of the enslaved.

The host of Poor press towards her.

1st Poor Man: Princess, your words are peace. The children of the
    poor pray for you.
2nd Poor Man: You are good. Let us kiss your feet.
3rd Poor Man: *kneels down*] You have helped us. We'd give our
    last crust to bring forth flowers round your grave.
Antigone: Stand up! I am your own kind.
    I am Antigone—
    A puny being that sinks back weak on the path she
        has traced
    Before the great shadow of death.
A Warrior: *roughly to the poor*] Back! Scum.
Antigone: You who shout in the chill of space:
    Where is your pity? You are poorer
    Than any, because you can no longer weep.
Voices: Let her be silent!
More Voices: Let her speak!
Antigone: Friends!
    I stood on the ramparts at nightfall. Heavily
    Troops thundered up from afar,
    Equipment, horses trotting. The night was bright,
    The canopy of heaven studded with panoply of
        battle;
    White chariots raced across Orion.
    Then the clouds parted and I saw
    Fiendish comets plummet earthwards,
    The elements spun, a hurricane of fire

Whirled up the lava of ultimate destruction—
But they were deflected, for Man was entrenched in
  power.
And again I saw the oceans stand still,
Shattered ships sink, houses fall in flames—
Mankind gone mad.
The glass mountain of the ages cracked:
I saw murder at the heart.
Mortal fear spread around me,
Lest each might be his neighbour's death;
Lest the great canals we built in the desert
Should observe our end with scorn,
Lifeless matter on the ruins of life.
I wanted to scream out a warning: cease, Man!
You err, you are deceived.
Unite, lift up your hearts,
Become brothers—
Then I saw my own brother fling
The fiery torch against the walls of the city,
I veiled my face, climbed down
And knew that I am only a woman.

The Citizen: She is right.—She accuses herself!

The Woman: If all die—where does that leave us?

The Warriors: Enough of killing.—Make peace at last.

The Youths: Speak on, Antigone.—Speak!

Antigone: I gave my brother back to the earth
And with you I celebrate resurrection.
Now we are brothers in suffering!
Now I know women can be immortal,
When they water the senseless ways of men
From the pitcher of love,
When help springs
From the tears of their poverty,
When the deed of the living heart
Makes walls of hostility tumble.

The People: Long live Antigone!

Antigone: Brothers!
I speak to you widows and orphans,
Who return home to your lonely dwellings,

	Where the sighs of the slain
	From the tear-stained stones of the hearth
	Startle your evening dream:
	Do you want your children,
	Bemused by cries of battle-glory,
	To share your wretched fate?
The People:	No!
Antigone:	Then go. Follow my example.
	Birth and death is reconciliation!
Shouts:	She shall not die!
Many Shouts:	She shall live!
The People:	Creon!

Scene 5

Creon:	*stands, suddenly illuminated, before the platform of the palace]*
	Why this noise?
The People:	Antigone must live!
Creon:	*takes one step forward]* I hear many mouths instead of one;
	If it were only one I should have it whipped
	Till the tongue spurted blood.
	You down below:
	Who do you think you are, pigs,
	To call me forth with your grunts?
The People:	She is innocent.
Creon:	Since when?
An Old Man:	She has atoned for the crime of her brother.
	Judge her not!
Creon:	Doddering fools, your graves stand open ready.
	Climb in and die!
A Woman:	She is a woman like us. She is no slut.
Creon:	I'll shut you up in your houses
	And see you starve.
	Rabble! All you want is to live for lust
	And rule men with your swelling bellies.

> Commit excess in your own beds,
> Not here before the house of the king.

Growing indignation.

Chorus of the Poor: *quiet song*]
> Peace to all sorrows
> Peace to all need
> The dawn of new tomorrows
> Already bids us heed.

Creon:
> From today the tribute is doubled.
> Work if you would eat.

He catches sight of ANTIGONE.

> Why do you stand and stare?
> Seize her! Take her to the place I commanded.

Antigone: *stands alone on the steps opposite him*]

> Kill me, kill me!
> Truth will come,
> To smash your might.

Creon:
> Take her out of my sight.
> I shall strike her dead!
> I shall send her myself to join the shades
> Who dolefully howl in the depths.

Antigone:
> Your might is a thing of the past.
> Your world is no more.
> From the depths of the rock I have hewn your people.
> Now it is my people!
> An end to serfdom:
> We fear it not!

Creon:
> Bury her alive!
> Anyone who brings her food will share her fate.
> Ere three days pass
> She will gnaw at stones.
> Seize her! [*Silence*].

Antigone:
> Will no-one seize me? Men—:
> I have softened your hearts.
> I will starve for you. I will bleed for you.

Thus I believe can good come to pass!
The rivers burst open. Love has conquered.
God's grace is with us.

Creon: *bellowing*] Who resists my command?
Move, will you!

Nobody moves.

Creon: *pulls out his whip, cracks it, then holds it aloft*]

Horsemen!!

Trumpet signals off-stage. Warriors on horse-back charge into the arena from all sides, riding the screaming people down. One leader pulls up his horse at the foot of the steps, snatches up ANTIGONE, *throws her backwards across the horse, races out with her, centre. Her hair trails on the ground. Death-screams.—Darkness.*

ACT III

The palace is dark. Moonlight. The tomb in the arena becomes light. Steps lead down into the vault. Armed men bring on ANTIGONE *left, in chains. They take off her fetters and go away.* HAEMON *detaches himself from the group and remains behind.* ANTIGONE *stands with her back towards him, close by the tomb.*

Scene I

HAEMON. ANTIGONE.

Haemon:	Antigone!
Antigone:	Is it you, Haemon?
Haemon:	Yes, it is I.
Antigone:	There are spies. The light will betray you. Follow me not!
Haemon:	I hate you.
Antigone:	*turns round*].
Haemon:	You have given your heart to a dead man.
Antigone:	We stand by my grave. Yet I am not purified, If I can still be hated.
Haemon:	You have lain in my arms. You are only a woman. I would have women whipped, Be victorious in battle. Kings shall acclaim me. Manhood shall gleam from my sword.
Antigone:	What do you know of me! Is this you, Haemon, This strange voice my heart hears not?
Haemon:	Love only him who is dead! I will live for my greater glory. Women are for love.
Antigone:	What is love?
Haemon:	Love is glory.

Antigone:	Aid to the weak, struggle for the world—
	Love is humanity!
Haemon:	The humblest men kneel down before you.
	Why cannot I?
Antigone:	King's son, accept your common humanity.
	Remember when your stars ascend
	That you are a mother's son.
Haemon:	Why must I hate you?
Antigone:	*silently takes one pace nearer*]
Haemon:	*trembling*] Speak one word!
Antigone:	Your heart is pure.

He sinks to the ground.

You will understand my work,
You will confess my name,
You will weep for yourself and for me.
Your soul is the world's image.

She places her hands upon him.

I would stay awhile with you
Before my flame expires,
Protect, serve you,
Be sister to your sufferings.
You were my guide;
You showed me freedom's pinnacles.
Already I dare to hope!
I love you
And leave you behind, friend.

Haemon:	I shall save you!

Exit left.

Scene 2

Ismene:	*from right*] I slipped through the guards.
	They sleep. Not one keeps watch.
	Come!
Antigone:	Whither?
	No river will quench the flame
	Of vengeance that burns in me.

Ismene:	Escape!
Antigone:	Here I stay.
Ismene:	You have done enough.
Antigone:	Am I to live Until slain by murderers?
Ismene:	You will not change the world Nor change wrong to right.
Antigone:	Goodness is better than prudence!
Ismene:	What do you intend?
Antigone:	To go on to the end So that light may dawn. As long as I live, I must be mortal.

She stretches out her hands.

O feel that we are women!
You are close to me.

They hold each other in tight embrace.

Ismene:	Are there not men too?
Antigone:	On the broad plain The men are led to slaughter.
Ismene:	Who is left?
Antigone:	You and I
Ismene:	Alas, mere women.
Antigone:	You women, enslaved and subjugated, Break free from the confines of your sex! Go hence and sacrifice yourselves.
Ismene:	Will God let us be worthy?
Antigone:	My deed has made you so.
Ismene:	Will all be worthy?
Antigone:	Yes, all, all—
Ismene:	We shall fight for you!

Exit right.

Scene 3

| Antigone: | *alone*] You who lie dead in your great burial hall,
Distant soul, uncertain light: |

What must I do,
Till free from pleasure, free from pain,
I can join you there below?
What can I do to make all believe me,
What sacrifice is great enough?
When lovers tremble at fate's touch in spring,
Who will say: Antigone—
You helped us. We believe you!
I am weak, so weak in the face of death.
Speak from the tomb. Answer me.

Silence.—The tomb darkens.

Scene 4

The palace becomes light, the arena is dark.

HAEMON. CREON.

Haemon:	I heard what happened.
Creon:	What do you want to know?
Haemon:	Right and wrong.
Creon:	You love her still?
Haemon:	Antigone!
Creon:	She lives no more.
Haemon:	What had she done?
Creon:	Ask my people.
Haemon:	They say—
Creon:	What do they say?
Haemon:	That she is in the right.
Creon:	So the falsehood grows even from her grave.
	I have crushed her, an animal
	That stabs me in the back.
	Do you likewise.
Haemon:	Yet I love her!
Creon:	The slut!
Haemon:	She is a woman.
	I have been taught to respect women.
Creon:	We are men and do not fear women.

Haemon:	Give me Antigone!
	Though she has transgressed I shall save her.
	I shall make her your most faithful follower.
Creon:	Am I to accept a transgressor?
Haemon:	You do not believe me?
Creon:	She is paying for what she has done.
Haemon:	Antigone will be my wife.
Creon:	A corpse?
Haemon:	She is innocent!
Creon:	I have heard that before.
Haemon:	Hear it from the lips of all!
Creon:	Who is master?
Haemon:	A great king kills a woman.
Creon:	Love leads you astray.
Haemon:	Are you human?
Creon:	King first.
	Why do you threaten me?
Haemon:	I warn you.

Exit through the palace.

Scene 5

Noises from below.

Creon:	*takes a step forward and stares into the darkness]*
	Die, little birth,
	For the bronze tablet of the great purpose
	I rule. I am in the right.

The noises increase. Tumult.

Creon:	*flies into a rage]* Captain!
Captain:	*steps out of the palace]* Lord?
Creon:	What is this noise.
Captain:	There is unrest outside among the people.
	Haemon is among them.
Creon:	Who?!
Captain:	Your son.
Creon:	*angrily]* Seize him!

Captain:	There is a shield of men around him.
Creon:	Do all the dogs conspire against me?
Captain:	Haemon—
Creon:	What is he doing?
Captain:	He is stirring up trouble.
	He is inciting the mob.
Creon:	And?
Captain:	He says you are a murderer.
	They follow him.
Creon:	Where are the horsemen?
Captain:	Mutinous rabble, I fear!
Creon:	Coward!
Captain:	*draws his sword*] As long as I live, king—
Creon:	Get out and fight!
Captain:	Shall I give the order for action?
Creon:	Killing—no!
	What if they find the two of us?
	What then?
Captain:	*goes pale*].
Creon:	It could cost you dear!
	Listen!
	When I raise my arm—like this:
	Set fire!!
Captain:	Fire . . . ?
Creon:	The whole city must burn.
Captain:	I can see them run!
Creon:	I'll teach them rebellion!
	All against one. Me against you!

Climax in the tumult. Hurricane.

Creon:	*leans forward into the darkness*] Come on. Come on!
	Whips out!
	Elephants! I'll trample you underfoot.
	Mine is the power!

Scene 6

Tiresias:	*in the audience, spotlighted*] Creon!
Captain:	*falls to his knees*] Tiresias, the seer.

Creon:	*clenches his fist at him*] Be gone, ghost!
Captain:	The voice of the eternal—
Creon:	*kicks the* CAPTAIN *down the steps into the darkness*]
	Get you into the bottomless pit!
Tiresias:	Creon, hear me.
	I am one hundred years old.
	I see the deeds of men.
Creon:	Why do you cross my path?
Tiresias:	Bow
	Before the Almighty.
Creon:	I, king, kneel before a hoary old man?!
	I'll have you shorn, and sent
	To join the moles.
Tiresias:	Vengeance is His.
Creon:	I bring it to pass.
Tiresias:	King!
	Woe betide you if you commit injustice.
	The hour of the damned is nigh.
	Beat on your breast, before it is too late.
	Cry for mercy!
Creon:	Black claw, you do not have me by the throat.
	I am still not crushed.
	Here I stand—
	And call to all points of the compass:
	What I ordain comes to pass!
Tiresias:	The mountain of death is higher than your palace.
	Already blood rises.
	Leap—for the last stone of your dominion.
	Pride goes before a fall.
Creon:	Liar!
	Only the people's stupidity
	Keeps your empty mind alive.
	Wither and die in the sand—
	No angel will bear you up to heaven.
Tiresias:	Creon, see me for what I am!
	Do not heap corpse upon corpse.
	Have mercy!
Creon:	*raises his fists*] So help me God!
	I am the master.

144

When the screams of the mutilated shrill,
When cities go up in smoke,
Mothers whimper:
Yet shall I wield the scourge,
Till the last enemy writhes at the stake,
The last thief, the last robber,
The whore, the traitor—
Till the iron chariot
Of Justice rolls over my city.

Tiresias: Then fall, accursed king—
Arise, all ye crucified!
All you slaughtered, wretched dead,
Strike him to the quick!

*The arena is suddenly flooded with light. Heaps of dead.
People with gaping wounds. Women, men with knives
in their chests. Demented bleating like animals. Smashed
limbs. Children stumble among the bodies.*

Shout: Creon!
Creon: *screams*] Ah . . .
Bestial howling, general surge towards him.
Creon: *mumbles through his teeth*] I do not know you—
A Madman: Don't know us? Don't know us?
Fine sir! King of the Crows! Hoho!
Creon: *flings his hands before his face*] Oh, terror!—Away!
A Cripple: My leg!
Bleeding Man: *whimpering*] Oh—
A Whore: Come to bed!
A Dying Man: *groaning*] Water!
Children: *searching among the dead*] Father! Father!
All: Murderer!
Creon: *falls on his knees, roars*] I am guilty.
I was wrong!

The arena becomes dark.

Voice of Tiresias: King of Thebes!
His is the power!!

145

F

Scene 7

Creon: *comes to*] What was that? Black Magic?
         Bodies with knives in them?
         What are the children calling among the dead?

         He stares at his hands.

         Hands, stained with blood!
         Fall from me, tattered flesh!

         He plunges his teeth into it.

         Let it be dark!
         Lighting dims.

         The king is fallen—
         Who laments?
         Silence.

         Beat on, heart—
         The cold of the battlefield,
         The horror of the dead.
         Hither, bodyguard, rampart of steel!
         Does no-one come? Am I to suffocate?

         Almost total darkness. He stands silhouetted on the ramp.

         I do not want to die. Death comes creeping.
         Darkness. I will atone.
         I smell the dead.
         Vengeance comes down upon me.

         *Distant roll of drums. One single trumpet note. He flings
            up his arms.*

         Day of Judgment! The trump.
         One day more! One hour more!
         I cast myself down. I pray.
         Help me, God!
Shout: *off-stage*] Antigone!
Creon: Antigone shall live!

         *Crescendo of voices and instruments to a climactic chord.
            Darkness.*

146

ACT IV

The Burial Place becomes light.

Scene 1

Antigone: *alone*] Because I lived and raised my head
To the voice of the eternal spirit,
Because I live and am a mother:
All men are my children.
I was created. Hence I may believe.
My sufferings are over. My life is beautiful.

She lays down her jewellery before the burial place.

But what if my face hardens at the last?
God!
Here by my brother's grave
Let me soar up to grace.
I have done what I can. My work is finished.

She takes a torch and lights it.

You gave me love for mankind;
I return it
Thousandfold before Your throne.
From on high
I shall see suffering in the dwellings of the multitude
And descend.
I shall come back,
And search the earth for unburied dead.
Mankind! A thousand years from now
I shall still be among you.

*She strides down into the vault.—Complete darkness.
Only the torch burns.*

Chorus: *from afar*] In the dark night
He succoured you.

Burial place and arena become light. ISMENE comes to the
    burial place.

Chorus: nearer] He will raise you
                From your burial place.
Ismene: enters the vault. Screams. Rushes out] Dead!!

                People crowd in.

The People: murmuring] Dead!?
Ismene: straightens up, rigid] Citizens of Thebes! Antigone is
                dead. Come to the burial place. She died for you!

                She collapses. Silence.—More people.

A Woman: There are her bracelets and rings.
2nd Woman: She has bequeathed them to us.
3rd Woman: Then take them!

                They rush at the jewellery, fighting among themselves.

A Citizen: Silence, you women. Think of the dead!
A Girl: peers into the burial place out of curiosity] There she is!
Many Women: Where?

                Crowding in front of the tomb.

Voices: She has hanged herself.—By her veil.—Over her
                brother.
A Citizen: Cut her down!

                Women enter the vault.

Voice: Poor woman!
Muffled Voice: Creon!

                A woman comes out of the burial place.

A Girl: Speak, how does she look?

                Second woman comes.—Murmuring.

The Woman: An angel has caressed her.
The People: Peace!

                Some kneel.—Many weep.

Scene 3

Commotion. CREON *enters centre with retinue.*

Creon:	Where is Antigone? I come to save her.
Voice:	Too late.
Creon:	Who speaks here?
Voice:	Death!
Creon:	*registers horror; stands petrified*].

Scene 4

Haemon: *with a host of youths*] Antigone! Freedom draws nigh.

He comes to the burial place and looks inside.

Who has done this thing?

Silence.

A Woman: Do not disturb her peace!

The youths lower their swords.

Haemon: It is over.

He falls against the wall of the burial place.—Silence.

Creon: *takes one pace nearer*].

Captain: Make way for the king!

Haemon: *starts up wildly, sees* CREON *approaching*]
Halt, murderer—the grave is mine.
Away!

He thrusts at him with his sword. Misses.

Creon: *without moving*].

Haemon: Die your own death.

The sword falls to the ground.

Voice: Antigone!

Haemon: *shattered*] Take the sin from me!
The hand with the sword of the judge
Withers.

149

He takes the torch from the grave.

Sister!
You have saved me from guilt.
Hatred is extinguished.

He flings the torch down before CREON's *feet. It goes out.*

I cast off honour and glory.
Weep—
Small voice in the evening sea—

He sits down on the steps and stabs himself.

Scene 5

Threatening silence.

A Voice: Your son is dead.
2nd Voice: Go to his dead body!
3rd Voice: King over dead bodies!
Many Voices: Murderer!—Jackal!
A Youth: *from the group about* HAEMON]
                       The first man of the new earth
                       Is converted by her grave.
A Voice: *loudly*] Stones for bread!
Echo: Stones—
Many Voices: Stone him!
2nd Youth: He died for her. The emptiness of death
                       Points the accusing finger at
                       The might of the living.

Shrill whistles.

Shout: Death to the murderer!
3rd Youth: The evil one lives. The good ones died.
                       Who may still say: I am a man?
A Woman: Speak, Creon!
2nd Woman: Why speak you not?
The People: Speak!
Creon: *petrified*].

An Armed Man: *raises his sword against the shouters*]
A Voice: Blood!

               Tumult.

The Mob: At him!

               They rush at the warrior.

Captain: To the king!

               *The guard surrounds him. He stands in the centre.
                 Scornful laughter.*

Shouts: Strike him dead!

               The wall round CREON *wavers. Trumpet call off-stage.
                 Glow of fire.*

A Voice: Fire!

               All turn round and stiffen. One section runs.

Many Voices: Fire!

               Fire burns more brightly.

Shout: Help!
Many Voices: The houses—the children—on fire.

               They rush for the exits.

The People: Save us!

               Clouds of smoke. Crackle.—Only the squad round CREON
                 remains.

Captain: *steps into the circle to* CREON] The flames fly!
               They never touch a king.
Creon: *stiffens, turns to go. The circle around him moves. He
                 looks back*]
               Bring my dead son's body!

               *They wrap a black cloth round the corpse and lift it.
                 All exit.—Glow of fire.—Darkness.*

ACT V

The palace is brightly lit. The arena in darkness. The steps illuminated.
EURYDICE *with her retinue enters from the gate.*

Scene 1

EURYDICE. LADIES-IN-WAITING.

1st Lady:	The flames of the great fire Have reduced the city to ruins.
Eurydice:	Where is Creon?
2nd Lady:	The King, your Lord, Went to the burial vault.
Eurydice:	Bid him come to me. I would open the great halls of the citadel As refuge for the homeless.

One Lady goes off.

1st Lady:	*looks out*] The forests are a-flame. Showers of sparks fly to the westering sky. Grey clouds billow. Fierce heat melts the towers.

Dull crash. Screams.

2nd Lady:	The roof of the temple is collapsing!
3rd Lady:	The fire draws closer.
Eurydice:	Where is my son?

Pause.

2nd Lady:	They rescue those buried by the rubble.
3rd Lady:	Many are burned to ashes.
Eurydice:	Go down, bring help to the sufferers. I will wait here for Creon And distribute the treasures of the citadel To the destitute.

All leave her except two ladies.

1st Lady:	A shriek of horror echoes through the flames—
Herald:	*appears in the entrance*].
Eurydice:	What is it?
Herald:	Antigone is dead!

An ancient crone, bent, mummified, crawls up the steps on hands and knees.

Mummy:	Your Majesty!
Eurydice:	Who calls?
Mummy:	My grandchildren are being roasted in the fire.
Eurydice:	Who are you?
Mummy:	I am a living skeleton. Burnt yellow by the heat.
Eurydice:	An animal!

She turns away filled with fear.

Mummy:	Queen! Here are worms. I am food for graves.
	Sits down on the steps, fumbles in her hair.
	When I beg you offer stones.
Eurydice:	*takes a cushion, descends one step and gives it to her.*
Mummy:	I give thanks for a soft pillow. Fire is lovely. Fire is warm.
1st Lady:	A pall of smoke.

Screams.

2nd Lady:	The flames! They are quite near.—
1st Lady:	*clinging to her*] Help, Your Majesty!

Crackles of flames by the steps.

Eurydice:	It is the end of the world.

The platform fills. The LADIES-IN-WAITING *come back.*

The Ladies:	We cannot help.
Eurydice:	Where is Creon? Where is my son?
A Voice:	They have not been seen.

Silence.

Eurydice:	Such suffering!

Gust of wind and sheet of flame over the citadel.

Herald: *behind the scenes*] Tiresias has died in the flames.

            Outcry.

1st Lady: The wind disperses the flames.
2nd Lady: The fire moves back to the plain.

            The flames fade.

Herald: *behind the scenes*] The citadel is saved.

            People stand on the steps.

A Girl: *roams around*] Where is my father?
An Old Man: My house in ashes. My bread burned. Where am I
            to live! What am I to eat? I am seventy years old.
A Half-naked Man: Give me a shirt! I freeze. Cover my nakedness!
A Charred Man: *whimpers*] Ah—ah—
The Girl: Has anyone seen my father?
Muffled Voice: *below*] We are consumed.
An Old Woman: *wanders about with a pot*] I dig and dig—for pots
            and pearls. Who has money? Who will buy?

            She rattles pearls in the pot.

A Mother: *holds up a charred human leg*] Your Majesty! Here is my
            child's leg. It was lying in the flames in the kitchen.
Voices: *murmuring*] No food—no home—we are poorer than
            rats.
A Voice: *shrilly*] See how the rich live!
Eurydice: I am not rich. Sorrow is the lot of a queen
            Who goes into the hovels of the poor,
            Gives alms, kneels to pray
            For the good of her people.
            Come closer. I cannot wake the dead
            Nor rebuild the houses in the city;
            At best I can only
            Feel with you how poor I am.
A Man of the People: We are weak. A human herd,
            Let us move out into the great forests
            In the face of God, and accuse.
            Look—

154

> *A shrouded bier is pushed in. He rips the cover off.*
> *A charred body lies there.*

Look here!
You have robbed us, maltreated us,
Abused us—
We too are human beings!

Shout: A curse upon the murderer!
The Man of the People: There is nothing left for us on this soil
  Before the throne of the mighty.
  We will creep into the valleys,
  Eat grass like cattle.
  But there, queen,
  Keep your hand from our lives.
  Remain behind,
  Rule in your citadel.
Eurydice: *discards the royal robe and stands in simple black dress*].
The Man of the People: Say farewell at the gate!
  Lost homeland, city in ashes.

Scene 2

> *Movement on the platform. The women draw back.*
> ISMENE *comes slowly through the gate.*

Eurydice: Ismene! Where is Creon?
Ismene: *shakes her head to indicate that she does not know*]
Eurydice: Poor thing!
Ismene: *tries to speak, shakes her head again. Points finger mutely off stage*].
Eurydice: What is wrong with her?
Ismene: *points to her mouth. Utters an incomprehensible sound*].
Eurydice: What does she say?
A Voice: She is mute!
Ismene: *utters a tiny, whimpering sound*].
Eurydice: Not yet enough! More still—!
Ismene: *steps hesitantly up to the queen, takes from her bosom a bloody knife and presents it to her*].

155

Eurydice: *shrieks*] Haemon's knife! Haemon!
         He lives no more—

         She reels. Ladies support her. All turn away. Silence.

The Man of the People: God's judgment on royalty!
Eurydice: *sobbing*] Haemon, my son!
A Woman: Our sons too are dead.
Eurydice: Haemon!!
An Old Woman: Poor Queen!
Eurydice: Away, flee!
         This place is a waste land!
         Murder holds sway.
Many Women: Sister!
Eurydice: *speaks to the Ladies-in-Waiting*]
         Mortal things are spent.
         Light the candles!

         *She leaves; the ladies follow her.—The ramp is empty;
         the gate closes. The arena becomes light.—People.*

The Man of the People: Palaces totter. Might has had its day.
         He who was great plunges to his doom,
         The gates thunder shut.
         He who possessed all has lost all;
         The slave in the sweat of his hands
         Is richer than he.
         Follow me! I will lead you.
         The wind rises from the ruins.
         The new world dawns.
A One-armed Man: My arm was smashed in the war. I can work
         with the other.
A Blind Man: My eyes are blind. I will teach children.
A One-legged Man: My leg was crushed. I will work at the loom.
The Man of the People: Come, all of you!
         You shall work. You shall live.
         Bread and fruit for all.
         The blood-letting is done.
         War dies away.
         Peoples extend the hand of friendship.

Chorus: Why do you hesitate?
                 The way is prepared.
                 Set your feet on the upward path.
The Man of the People: Follow me! Farewell to the dead!
                 The living give you greeting—

                 *A part of the crowd has formed up about him. They
                 march out with him through the centre of the arena.*

Scene 3

                 The gate of the palace opens. CREON *appears with retinue.
                 Warriors carry on the body of* HAEMON *in its black
                 cloth and lay it down on the ramp, right in front of the
                 steps.—Silence.*

Creon: Men of Thebes!
                 I come to sit in judgment on the guilty.
                 God's hand lies heavy upon us.
                 Some vile fire-raiser has set fire to the city.
                 He is amongst us. Let him step forward.

                 Nobody moves.

Creon: *half-turns*] Forward! Who gave the sign?
Captain: *steps forward*] I did, my Lord.
Creon: *to the people*] Behold: this man!—
                 What is to be done with him?
Voice: Have him impaled!
Creon: Throw him in chains.

                 This is done.

Captain: *shouts*] I did it at the king's command!!
Creon: Silence, cut-throat!
Captain: On this very spot
                 He ordered me
                 To set fire to the city.
Creon: Did I raise my arm—thus?

                 He does it.

157

Captain:	Your life was in danger!
Creon:	Did I give the sign?
Captain:	*falls at his feet*] Mercy—
Creon:	Remove his chains. Like a beast
	Man follows his wild thirst for blood.
	The deed is other than the mind envisaged.
	Indict me. Indict God!

The CAPTAIN *rushes off. Chains dragging behind him.*

Creon: It was to me
The thought occurred—so I am guilty.
I had to exercise the power of the king.
Freedom is stronger than glory
And the dead letter of the law.
A ruler of men must know
Good and evil and choose the better.
I heard the confused march of the spirits;
It was a different spirit that spoke to me.
Yes, I am guilty! The magnitude of what one must do
Even error itself, engages the wheel of the world
And drives it on between light and shadow,
Temptation, fate, duty and destruction.

He stops.—The mob presses forward to listen.

Because I was the mightiest in my kingdom
I will confess that I am guilty.

He steps up to the body of his son.

What throne and sovereignty created
Crumbles before this plain, black cloth.
Here is the grave of mankind—
The bitter fulfilment: death.

Chorus of Virgins: *by the grave of* ANTIGONE]
Thanks Be!
Day is breaking.
Stones send forth flowers on the graves.

Creon: You hosts in the deep!

The day is come, when the barrier falls.
When the king is one with his people
Before the throne of justice.
I go now to atone for my crimes
Into the desert, into the virgin forest,
Far from you all. We shall meet no more.

Funeral music.—The gates of the palace open. Candles
burn. In the background the catafalc, on which EURYDICE
lies in state. Around it kneel her ladies.

Muffled Voice: The queen is dead!
Creon: *stares at the bier*] Three dead freeze into my heart.
           Their icy fingers
           Tear my flesh from me
           Piece by piece.
           Now I lie helpless in the field,
           Like the dead foe.

He unbuckles his sword.

Put off at the feet of your poor son
The symbol of your grandeur.
My wife, now here at rest—
The day grows lonely round me.

He moves forward to the top of the steps.

The path down to you, my brothers,
Is but a short way past the grave.
A few steps still separate us. Already the hand
Of the timeless clock draws nearer.
But one day when the dead awaken,
When the immortals
Enter their realm,
I shall return to my stars,
I—
Who knew much and did much
For good and evil: a Man!

He strides slowly down the steps from the palace into the arena. The mob parts. He passes through to the burial place, takes the golden circlet from his head, and places it on top of the vault. Exit centre. The music breaks off.—Silence.

Scene 4

Voice:	The king is gone!
2nd Voice:	We have no king any more!
3rd Voice:	We are free!!
One from the Mob:	Why don't we storm the citadel!
Rabble:	Money—wine!

They press forward. Those standing in front are trampled on. Screams. Some come up the steps with raised fists. They are on the ramp. They stop before the coffin.

Shout:	*below]* Forward!

They stand before the gates.

A Man:	*lifts up the body of* HAEMON *and flings it down].* Down with princes!

Thunder and lightning.

Voice from the Tomb:	People, Fall down— God has passed judgment.

They turn full of horror. The clenched fists sink paralysed. They fall down, beat their heads against the ground.

Pray!
O Man!
Guilty!
Ephemeral!

They raise their hands in supplication.—Darkness.

END

HINKEMANN

A TRAGEDY
IN THREE ACTS

by

Ernst Toller

Written in Niederschönenfeld penitentiary

1921-22

Translated by J. M. Ritchie

HINKEMANN

People of the tragedy

HINKEMANN

GRETA HINKEMANN, *his wife*

OLD MRS. HINKEMANN

PAUL GROSSHAHN

MAX KNATSCH

PETER IMMERGLEICH

SEBALDUS SINGEGOTT

MICHEL UNBESCHWERT

FRANKIE, *Greta's girl friend*

SHOWMAN

Various workers, male and female
Various characters of the German street scene

Scene: About 1921, Germany

NOTE: In the original German text HINKEMANN is referred to as Eugeni. This has been changed to 'Adam' in the English version.

ACT I

Scene 1

The stage suggests: working-class kitchen-living room. GRETA *is busy about the cooker.* HINKEMANN *comes in. Sits down at the table. His right hand rests on the table clutching a small object. He stares hard at this hand.*

HINKEMANN *speaks neither 'fluently' nor 'rhetorically'. At all times his speech has the ponderous groping quality of the elemental soul.*

GRETA: Did my mother give you coal?

HINKEMANN: [*does not reply*].

GRETA: Adam! . . . I'm asking you, did my mother give you coal . . . Answer me . . . You'd think he wasn't even in the room! . . . Adam, say something . . . I'm at my wits' end! Not a stick! not a lump of coal! . . . Adam, do I have to burn the bed?

HINKEMANN: Such a little thing . . . such bright colours . . . just feel its heart beating; . . . you can feel it in your hands. In darkness now. Forever in darkness.

GRETA: What have you got in your hand, Adam?

HINKEMANN: How can you stand there? And not let everything drop out of your hands? Can't you feel a great darkness coming over you? A little creature, a thing of this earth like you or me . . . full of life only minutes ago . . . cheep, cheep. You know how they sing in the mornings? Cheep, cheep . . . that's joy at seeing the light . . . cheep . . . And now! now! I came into the room just as she was poking its eyes out with a red-hot knitting needle . . . [*Groaning out loud*] Oh! Oh!

GRETA: Who? Who?

HINKEMANN: Your mother. Your own mother. Fancy a mother poking out a canary's eyes with a red-hot needle, just because some rag of a newspaper said blind birds sing better . . . I flung the coal at her feet and the money she'd given me, Greta . . . I . . . thrashed your mother the same as you thrash a child that's cruel to animals . . . But then I let her go . . . something that came into my head made me stop. A horrible thought, horrible! Wouldn't I have done the same once? And thought nothing of it? What was an animal's suffering to me? Just an animal. You wring its neck, cut its throat, shoot it. So what. When I was fit I thought that was how things were. Now that I'm a cripple I *know*: It's something horrible! It's murdering your own flesh! Worse than murder! Torturing living flesh! . . . But in the old days . . . when you're sound in body you're blind!

GRETA: What have you done? . . . Now we haven't got a hope.

HINKEMANN: But think: a mother poking a creature's eyes out. I can't get over it! I never will! I can't get over it!

GRETA: [*goes out*].

HINKEMANN: Poor little bird . . . we're mates . . . they've fixed us good and proper, you and me. Human beings did it. Human beings. We call them human beings; you'd call them devils if you could speak! . . . Greta! . . . She's gone. Probably a bit sick of our company. [*Hunts about for something*]. What about some crumbs . . . or a cage . . . a cage? So we can see each other's plight? . . . No, no, I won't be cruel. I'll play Fate

instead. A kinder fate than my own. Because I . . . I care . . .
I care . . .

HINKEMANN *rushes out. Comes back a few seconds later.*

HINKEMANN: Scrunch! A splatch of red on the wall . . . A few
feathers fly . . . All over! . . . Some little thing comes into
your head and your whole world totters! If somebody had
pointed out the likes of me in the old days, I don't know what
I'd have done. You can't tell what you would do in some
circumstances, you don't know yourself well enough . . .
Maybe I'd have laughed . . . maybe I'd have . . . laughed!
What about her? . . . Her mother poked a canary's eyes out
. . . what will she do, eh?

Laughs hysterically. Starts screeching a song.

Ah . . . Ah . . .

While he is singing, GRETA *comes into the room, looks at him in
horror. As if sickened by it, she holds her ears. Suddenly she sobs aloud.*

GRETA: Oh my God . . . Oh my God . . .

HINKEMANN: *catches sight of* GRETA *and turns on her in a burst of rage*]
What is it? . . . what are you howling at, woman? . . .
Answer me! . . . What are you bawling at, eh! . . . come
on! . . . Are you bawling because I . . . because you and me
can't . . . because people would point me out in the streets
like a clown, if they knew what was the matter with me?
Because some blasted hero's bullet made me a cripple . . . a
laughing-stock? Because you're ashamed of me? . . . Tell the
truth . . . the truth . . . whole world tottering . . . whole
world tottering . . . I must know the truth! [*Tenderly. Beseech-
ing*]. Why are you crying?

GRETA: I . . . I love you . . .

HINKEMANN: Are you sure it's love . . . or is it pity that makes
you shudder when you hold my hand?

GRETA: I love you . . .

HINKEMANN: You've had a dog since it was a pup . . . played
with it when you were a kid . . . a good animal, a faithful
beast . . . a dog that would never let anybody harm you . . .
now this dog begins to go mangy. His coat gets filthy, his eyes

run . . . you can't bear to touch him, he's so sickening . . . only, you see, you remember the dog he was in the old days, that used to look at you out of his wonderful, understanding eyes when life was getting you down a bit . . . And then you just can't bring yourself to have him put down . . . you even put up with him in the house . . . you even put up with him when he climbs onto your bed . . .

Screaming out.

Greta! Am I like that dog?

GRETA: *covers her ears in desperation*] I can't stand any more! I'll hang myself . . . gas myself! . . . I can't stand any more!

HINKEMANN: *helpless*] Greta, what's the matter? I won't touch you. I'm finished. A disease you don't talk about. A puppet that's been worked to death . . . The pension's too little to live on and just too much to die on . . . Greta, I'd be prepared to scab on my own work-mates, I'd even agree . . . to be a strike-breaker, a blackleg . . . If I only knew . . . what tortures me, really tortures me . . . is the thought . . . it's with me all the time like a bunch of red-hot pins jabbing, jabbing into me: you're nothing to your wife but a mangy old dog . . .

Softly, secretly.

And since this morning, Greta . . . after what happened at your mother's place, since I've had this idea in my head, this horrible idea haunting me, haunting me, haunting me . . . I see faces grinning at me . . . There's a gramophone at my ear like a sinister beast screeching out its tune: Silly old Adam! Silly old Adam! . . . And then suddenly I see you . . . You're all alone in the room standing by the window, and I go down the street . . . you hide behind the curtain . . . killing yourself laughing, laughing fit to burst . . .

After a few moments he says simply:

You couldn't do that to me, Greta, could you? You couldn't laugh at me?

GRETA: What can I say, Adam? . . . You don't believe me as it is.

HINKEMANN: Yes! Yes, I do, Greta! I could go mad with joy! I believe you! I'll get work! . . . Even if I have to crawl on all fours! . . .

PAUL *comes in.*

PAUL: Evening all.

HINKEMANN AND GRETA: Hullo, Paul.

PAUL: Bright lot you are, I don't think! I've come for a few laughs.

HINKEMANN: You don't need them, Paul! You're doing alright.
You've got your job: soon be a boss.

PAUL: Like hell! The new retrenchment policy will be the end of
my job! The working man is worse off than the beasts of the
field . . . at least they get fattened up, put out to pasture and
they're not slaughtered off till they're nice and fat, fat and
tender.

GRETA: How can you be guilty of such blasphemy? You're forgetting about the life hereafter.

PAUL: How can the likes of us forget? Supposing there is a hereafter,
a life of eternal bliss, the poor are bound to get there, (a) because
all the scraping and slaving never leaves them any time for
sinning and (b) because they have to have some reward for
providing their exploiters with a life of eternal bliss on earth
. . . Anyway I'm an atheist. Don't believe in God any more.
Which God, I ask you? The Jews' God? The heathens' God?
The Christians' God? The French God? The German God?

HINKEMANN: Maybe the whole lot of them got left behind on the
barbed wire entanglements . . . always sticking their noses
into wars.

GRETA: I have believed in a just God all my life, and nobody can
take that away from me.

PAUL: If God was just, he'd have to act just, Mrs. Hinkemann.
But how does he behave, the dear, good, just God? Eh? Do I
need to remind you? With God for King and Country, with
God for massacre, with God for super-God Mammon. Everything's the will of God. Seems as if, whenever our 'betters'
find it's not convenient or they're ashamed to say 'for my sake',
they say 'for God's sake'. Sounds better . . . people all fall for
it . . . I leave faith to them that make money out of it. The
likes of us are not fighting for the next world, we're fighting
for this one, we're fighting for humanity.

HINKEMANN: Fighting for humanity is all well and good. But for
factory machines . . . They crush our bodies before we're fully
grown. Every new working day is a nightmare, and when I

start work in the morning I can't imagine how anybody can stand the whole day. And when the hooter goes at the end of the day, I rush out the factory gates, like a mad thing!

PAUL: Machines don't bother me. I'm the boss, not the machine. When I'm standing at the machine a devil inside me starts up: 'You must show this slave who's boss!' And then I drive it screaming and whining and moaning to the absolute limit. I make it sweat blood . . . know what I mean . . . and I laugh, I love seeing it grind on shaking itself to death. So, my baby, I shout, you do what I say! Anything I say! And I stuff anything down its throat and make it turn out anything I want! What I want! Be a man, Adam, then you're on top.

HINKEMANN: *quietly*] Sometimes in this world you can become a God easier than a man.

GRETA: *stares fixedly at* PAUL] How fierce you can look.

PAUL: Aarh . . .

HINKEMANN: He can look fierce alright, but he doesn't get that from handling machines.

GRETA: Where then?

HINKEMANN: Where do you think? From handling women.

PAUL: What else is there in life for the workers? As soon as he's born the old man curses because there's another mouth to feed. He goes hungry to school in the morning and hunger tears at his guts when he goes to bed at night. Then he goes through the mill. He sells his strength like you'd sell petrol and he belongs to the capitalist, the boss. All he is now is a hammer, or a chair, or a steam-press, or a pen, or a what-have-you. That's the way it goes . . . What's the only pleasure that's left to him? LOVING! Nobody can poke their nose into that, can they?— LOVING! The only time he's free, the only time he can say to capitalist or cop: This is my home ground! Keep Out!!— LOVING!! Look, the rich have got so many things to keep them amused . . . holidays and music and books . . . but people like us? We may read a book once in a while, but not every day. We didn't learn enough in school, we haven't got the brains. Music? Wagner's all right, I suppose, but give me a bit of variety . . . or something light like 'The Merry Widow' . . . you know how it goes . . .

Singing the opening of 'The Merry Widow'.

'Vilja, oh Vilja' . . . or when you put your coin in the juke box and it plays something you can dance to . . . that's the stuff for me . . . For workers like us loving means one heck of a lot more than it does for the rich. For us it's . . . how can I put it . . . it's the stuff of life. Right, Adam?

HINKEMANN: You could be right . . .

PAUL: You're a married woman, Mrs. Hinkemann, so I can speak my mind with you. What would the likes of us get out of life if we couldn't have a woman every day.

HINKEMANN: *watches* GRETA *intently*].

PAUL: What do you say, Mrs. Hinkemann?

GRETA: What do I say? . . .

Shyly.

All women are not alike.

HINKEMANN: *leaping to his feet*] I'll get work, Greta, believe me . . . I want to be able to give you something for Christmas! . . .

PAUL: Waste of time.

HINKEMANN: Wait and see, Paul, my boy! Bye, Greta.

HINKEMANN *leaves the room. A few minutes' silence.*

PAUL: He's built like an all-in-wrestler. Shame nobody can find a use for him. And always sees the bright side. You must be very happy, Mrs. Hinkemann.

GRETA: *stares at him fixedly*] Yes.

PAUL: I'm always jealous of Adam when I see the two of you together.

GRETA: *puts her head in her hands and weeps*]

PAUL: What's wrong, Mrs. Hinkemann? . . . Did I say something wrong? You're crying . . . What is it then? . . . Will I go and get Adam? Maybe I can still catch him . . .

GRETA: *sobbing uncontrollably*] My head is splitting! . . . I'm going mad! . . . I just want to scream! . . . scream! . . .

PAUL: *anxiously*] Are you sick, Mrs. Hinkemann? Can I do anything for you? Or maybe you're pregnant? . . . It gets some women like that.

GRETA: Great God Almighty . . . pregnant . . .

Laughing hysterically

pregnant, when I feel like death.

PAUL: Is Adam not good to you? Does he beat you?

GRETA: I must tell somebody . . . I must . . . I must . . . I must . . . I'm so unhappy . . . my Adam . . . my Adam . . . my Adam, he's not a . . . he's not a man at all.

PAUL: Are you sure you're not sick, Mrs. Hinkemann? Maybe a bit feverish?

GRETA: Oh no . . . my Adam . . . my Adam was away at the war and they fixed him . . . and now he's a cripple . . . I'm so ashamed . . . I can't explain . . . Can't you understand, Mr. . . . he's not a real man any more . . .

Claps her hand over her mouth in horror at what she has done.

PAUL: *utters one short crude guffaw*]

GRETA: God! . . . What have I done? What have I said? How can you laugh at me . . . You ought to be ashamed! ashamed! I'd never have thought . . . never have dreamt you could do a thing like that.

PAUL: I'm sorry, Mrs. Hinkemann, it just slipped out . . . just slipped out . . . you just can't help yourself when you first hear it. [*Indignantly*] But that Adam is a selfish bloke! Holding on to you! He can't love you, if he did he'd let you go . . .

PAUL *begins to stroke her caressingly.* GRETA *leans up against him.*

GRETA: It's not so simple as you think, Mr. Paul. It's not easy to know what to do. One minute everything is bright, next minute black as pitch . . . I'm so sorry for him . . . What a man he used to be before the war. In his prime! But now . . . spends all his time brooding. He bickers with God and man . . . and when he looks at me I feel he wants to look right through me as if I was some kind of object and not a human being. And sometimes, I'm afraid of him . . . I can't stand him . . . it makes me sick to look at him! . . . [*Shuddering*] makes me sick! Oh my God! What's to become of us? . . .

PAUL: *becoming more and more tender*] Have a good cry, Mrs. Greta, just have a good cry . . . Tears you choke back lie heavy like stones on your heart, my dear departed mother used to say . . .

GRETA: You won't let on you know, Mr. Paul? I'd drown myself!

PAUL: Not a word, Greta. Not a single word. Don't worry on that score. I once did a month in prison because I'd promised to keep my trap shut . . . don't worry on that score . . . you're a young woman . . . look at me . . . you'll never last out another year, wearing yourself out fretting like this . . . little Greta . . . baby . . .

Kisses her.

GRETA: This is wicked . . .

PAUL: Wicked? How can it be wicked when it's only natural? . . . in the blood . . . Wicked is a word the priests and the capitalists like to juggle with . . . It would be wickedness to yourself if you were faithful to him when he's not a man at all. Anyway what's this faithful stuff. More religious mumbo-jumbo to keep the rabble quiet. They stopped believing in it themselves a long time ago. A friend of mine used to have a thing going with a banker's wife . . .

GRETA: There's somebody on the stairs . . . If it's Adam . . .

PAUL: I'd better be off then . . . Greta, what about coming round to my place sometime? You know where I live . . . No need to be scared, nobody ever comes near the place . . . You can get it all off your chest . . . if you see what I mean . . . you can have a good cry . . . Will you come?

GRETA: I don't know yet . . .

PAUL: Remember how we used to play together in the park and build castles in the sand pit? Remember, Greta? . . . I had my eye on you even in those days when you were just a kid . . . You'll come and see me, won't you, baby?

GRETA: *struggling with herself, shakes her head*].

PAUL: *with sudden brutality*] Stop pretending you don't want to . . . You'll come! . . .

GRETA: I . . .

PAUL: You'll come!

GRETA: All right . . .

PAUL: Right, Greta. Goodbye, baby.

PAUL *goes out.*

GRETA: *alone*] What's a poor woman to do.
Life is so difficult.

Curtain.

ACT II

Scene 1

The stage suggests the outside of a caravan. On a stump sits the owner surrounded by the various paraphrenalia of a travelling side-show. HINKEMANN *is standing in front of him.*

HINKEMANN: *pointing to a newspaper*] There!
SHOWMAN: What d'you mean . . . 'there!'
HINKEMANN: There it is in black and white

Reads slowly stressing every word

'Strong Man wanted for sensational turn. Liberal remuneration. Only first-class human material need apply'.
SHOWMAN: Oh, that. Step into the light, boy. [*Feels* HINKEMANN'S *muscles*] Biceps flabby . . . Chest . . . thighs . . . calves . . . flabby. But just what I'm looking for. Looks better than the real thing. *Looks* as strong as a bull. Fine! Great! You're hired! Shake!
HINKEMANN: And what do I have to do?
SHOWMAN: What? Easy as pie. Listen! People are not little white lambs. Only the pacifists think they are. Bad for business. People want to see blood!!! Blood!!! Two thousand years of Christianity can't change that! This is what my show caters for. So public and private interest go hand in hand. Get it? Not the faintest glimmer naturally.

Picks up a flute.

What's this? [*Plays a few notes on the flute*] Mush for old maids! Woodnotes wild! Coffee substitute with saccharin! Ugh! . . . What's this? [*Seizes two drum-sticks. Begins to beat a big drum*] Well, what is it? [*Drum roll*] What the public wants! [*Drum roll*] Intoxication! [*Drum roll*] Ecstasy! [*Drum roll*] Life!
HINKEMANN: Weren't you going to tell me? . . .

SHOWMAN: Just coming to it! On my left a cageful of rats! On my right a cageful of mice! Small fortune in it. Your turn: at every performance you take one rat and one mouse and tear a hole in their throats with your teeth; take a couple of sucks of blood. Flourish! Off! Audience goes crazy!

HINKEMANN: Live animals?! . . . No, sir, I can't do it.

SHOWMAN: Rubbish! Five pounds a day. All found. Only fifty minutes' work all told . . . What's wrong with it! All a matter of habit. Then there's the perks! You'll be swamped with women. You'll have to fling your scruples overboard. Maidenheads can be mended these days. There are specialists for everything.

HINKEMANN: *greedily*] Five pounds . . .

SHOWMAN: Swallowed the hook? Hahaha.

HINKEMANN: Horrible . . . li—ve . . . animals! . . .

SHOWMAN: Just try and get any other kind of work, man. Nothing doing! Hahaha! Either—or!

HINKEMANN: *choking*] It . . . is . . . only . . . for . . . my . . . wife . . . [*jerkily*] When somebody loves you! When you're afraid you might lose that little bit of love! There's not much love about for the likes of me! . . . Isn't there something else you could use me for, sir?

SHOWMAN: Either—or!

HINKEMANN: *stammering, almost whimpering*] Ooh . . . ooh . . . ooh . . . five pounds . . . ooh . . . the likes of me . . . likes of me! . . . Waltzing . . . spinning . . . spinning! . . . Round and round! . . . I'll do it, sir.

SHOWMAN: That's my boy! Royalty, Top Brass, Priests and Showmen—they're the real politicians: they know what the people want.

Stage darkens.

Scene 2

Faint candlelight. The silhouettes of PAUL *and* GRETA *appear against the back wall.*

PAUL: Love me?

GRETA: You. You.

PAUL: And Adam thinks . . .

GRETA: Don't let's talk about him! I hate him, hate him!

PAUL: Funny creatures women, . . . why didn't you run away right from the start, when he came back . . . when you found out?

GRETA: Oh, I don't know. I don't remember. I think I was ashamed to let anybody else know.

PAUL: Poor bloke really, when you think of it.

GRETA: Don't think of it. I don't want you to.

PAUL: After all, he is my friend.

GRETA: Don't! I tell you, don't!

PAUL: *after a while*] What happened the first night? Did he try?

GRETA: Oh, Paul . . . please don't talk about it!

PAUL: And if he was O.K. would you still come to me? . . . What are you getting up for? What are you doing?

GRETA: God strike you dumb! And me! And him! And everybody! Talking about it is the worst part of it!

Stage darkens.

Scene 3

The stage suggests: a show-ground. In front of a side-show whose brightly-painted walls shout louder than the din. Music from barrel-organ. Brass. On the platform in front of the booth a tattooed lady and HINKEMANN, *who is wearing flesh-coloured tights.*

SHOWMAN: *in hard, staccato voice*] Ladies and gentlemen! Step this way! Walk up, walk up! Stop! Look! Listen! Introducing, in the first part of our show: Manochia, the Tattooed Lady, with wonderful old masterpieces by Rembrandt, Rubens, etcetera . . . on the front-side of her naked body . . . and most avant-garde expressionistic, futuristic, dadaistic portraits of royalty . . . on the backside! You won't only see her arms, you won't only see her back, you will see every single part of her body which by civil and church law only ladies and gentlemen over the age of eighteen are permitted to behold . . . In addition, you will see a child being beheaded. A real live child! You have never seen the like before! You won't see this in Africa, you won't

174

see this in Asia, you won't see this in Australia, this can be seen only in Europe and America! As finale [*pointing to* HINKEMANN] Homunculus, the German Bull! Devours live rats and mice before the very eyes of our esteemed public! German heroism! German culture! German virility! German strength! All this personified. *The* favourite of the lovely ladies! Grinds stones to powder! Hammers nails through the thickest skull with his bare fists! He can strangle three-and-twenty men between finger and thumb! All flee before him. And all who flee must DIE by his hand! You can't say you've seen Europe till you've seen him. But we have more in store for you! Surprises under whose sheer transparent coverings I will not and cannot yet let you look. So—walk right up, ladies and gentlemen! We're not asking one shilling, we're not asking sixpence, threepence a head is what you pay today. Because we know every house will be a sell-out *threepence* a head is what we charge! So walk up, walk up! First come, first served! The orchestra is playing the overture! Artistes going backstage. [*Bell rings*] Have the correct change ready, please!

GIRL: *pointing at* HINKEMANN] How'd you like to feel his muscles, Theresa!

SECOND GIRL: Or touch his torso . . .

SHOWMAN: *who has heard every word*] Certainly, ladies, touch as much as you like! Absolutely nothing false! Nothing phoney! That's Homunculus, the incarnate might of the German Empire!

PAUL *and* GRETA *come on with arms round each other's waists. At first they don't look in the direction of the side-show. While they speak the din and noise from the side-show becomes inaudible. What people are doing is clearly intelligible from their dumb show.*

PAUL: Isn't life wonderful, Greta? Makes you want to shout for joy! Want to go on the roundabout, Greta? You can have anything you like now!

GRETA: It's all like a dream . . . like a fairy-story . . . after those six years of pain and worry and misery I was cowering there like a mouse that has crawled into its hole afraid to face the light of day. Not that I ask much from life . . . no need to think that . . . Any working-class girl's own family has shown her what's in store for her. If she's lucky life will be one long struggle and when she's too old for it she'll have her children to turn to. If she's not lucky, squabbles, fights, beatings. But I never imagined it could ever be like this! . . .

PAUL: This is the start of a new life.

GRETA: *tenderly*] Paul . . .

PAUL: What is it, Greta?

GRETA: Darling . . . [GRETA *kisses* PAUL *long and tenderly*].

PAUL: *with obvious self-satisfaction*] Hey! In front of all the people . . . not so shy now . . . I knew it . . . that shy business . . . it's all imagination . . .

The voice of the SHOWMAN *makes itself heard.*

SHOWMAN: Homunculus, the German Bull! . . .

His voice becomes inaudible again.

GRETA: Paul! Paul!

PAUL: What are you so excited about, Greta?

GRETA: Look over there, Paul! . . . Know who that is?

PAUL: Who?

GRETA: The Strong Man in tights?

PAUL: How should I know? Some bloke who works the shows. Here today, gone tomorrow.

GRETA: It's him!

PAUL: Who?

GRETA: Adam.

The voice of the SHOWMAN *can be heard again.*

SHOWMAN: Devours live rats and mice before the very eyes of the esteemed public. *The* German hero! The paragon of German manhood! Homunculus! Flex your muscles. Your attention— Ladies and gentlemen!

HINKEMANN *goes into a wrestling crouch and flexes his muscles. The* SHOWMAN'S *voice fades.*

PAUL: Did you ever see such a fraud! That supposed to be the German hero! A man with no . . . A eunuch . . . Hahahaha! Maybe that's what the home-front hero looked like. Maybe that's what the H.Q. wallahs, the pot bellies, the press boys, the profiteers, the glory-merchants, the arm-chair jingoists looked like! . . . That showman is making money out of a fake!

GRETA: Shut up . . . shut up . . . how can you be so heartless! What about me, what an awful woman this makes me. Worse than the lowest slut . . . she, poor creature, just sells her body: *I* sell my man . . .

PAUL: *holds her tight in his arms*] Stop shouting! Don't be so silly!

GRETA: Didn't you hear? He's eating live rats and mice! That man could never have hurt a fly. That man even struck my mother because she poked her canary's eyes out. That man wouldn't let me set mouse-traps in the kitchen—said it was a sin to hurt the mice so much . . . and here he is eating live rats and mice . . .

PAUL: Well, as from today you won't have to kiss him anyway!

GRETA: I'll kiss him . . . right now . . . on that stage . . . in front of everybody! What have I done to him! How could he help that bullet? It wasn't his fault! It was my fault for letting him go to war! His mother's fault! It's the times we live in that let things like that happen.

PAUL: Shut up! People are beginning to stare. Let's go. Maybe he can see you.

GRETA: I want him to see me, want him to see my shame! I want to fall on my knees before him: a god-forsaken creature. I'm a worm in his sight. Let me go, let me go to him!

PAUL: *holding* GRETA *close to his body*] And what if you feel sickened by him again?

GRETA: *simply*] Then I will love him all the more.

PAUL: *drags* GRETA *off with him*] You must be out of your mind, woman! Come on!

The voice of the SHOWMAN *can be heard again.*

SHOWMAN: Walk up! Walk up! Ladies and Gentlemen. You will be amazed!

The SHOWMAN *goes into the tent.*

ONE WORKING WOMAN: *to another*] Just because I'm taking these clothes to the pawnshop doesn't mean there's no more like them at home . . . And I've got a lovely veil, pure silk . . . handed down from my grandmother . . . but there's nothing else worth pawning . . . so it has to be the clothes . . . [*Walk past*].

177

G

PAUL *and* GRETA *on the other side of the stage.*

GRETA: *still held fast by* PAUL. *Struggling*] Nn . . . oo!

PAUL: You're not coming with me?

GRETA: Nn . . . o!

PAUL: And what happens when he finds out you're pregnant?

GRETA: He will forgive me . . . he is good . . .

PAUL: He'll beat you black and blue!

GRETA: This is how it has to be . . . Now I see God's will. I was wrong. God has not forsaken me. God's will for me is a life of atonement. I accept it humbly. I will serve Adam as if he were my saviour.

PAUL: I'll go and see him . . . right now . . .

GRETA: We'll both go and see him . . .

PAUL: And tell him you've been going with me . . .

GRETA: Why try to threaten me, Paul. Nothing can make me come with you. I never really called my life my own. When I was little I was always waiting for LIFE. Later on I saw it sometimes in the distance. But whenever I reached out to grasp it, I'd suddenly realise how rough and dirty my hands were and life always looked as if it was dressed in silk . . . and then I wouldn't have the nerve and I'd hide my hands under my apron. Why should everybody see my hands! Now I feel life itself would be dirty and not worth reaching out for.

PAUL: *with extreme annoyance because his vanity has been hurt*] Then bugger off, you snivelling cow! There's plenty more where you came from . . . I just need to bend my little finger . . . they'd swarm like bees . . .

They are swept off-stage by the crush.
The SHOWMAN *has stepped out of his tent.* HINKEMANN *with him.*

SHOWMAN: Step right up! Step right up! Ladies and gentlemen! Stop! Look! Listen! You will be amazed!

The stage darkens.

Scene 4

The stage suggests: Small working-class bar. A bustling buxom friendly barmaid serves behind the counter. Customers sit at bare wooden tables.

MAX, PETER, SEBALDUS *and others. Two workmen, a* SLATER *and a* TILER, *are standing at the bar. Even before the curtain goes up voices can be heard quarrelling.*

SLATER: Not if there was a hundred revolutions! That's one thing revolutions can't change! Interior decorating is better than house-painting, publishing better than printing, linotype better than typing, copper work better than boilermaking, chauffeuring better than van-driving. *We'll* always work with slates and *you'll* never get beyond tiles.

TILER: Stupid conceit! Rot! Snobs! How can we sit here and drink with the likes of you! We may be nothing but scruffy tilers and not noble slaters like your lordship! But we're proud of it! Tilers and proud of it!

SLATER: Working with slates is an art! Laying tiles is just labouring!

TILER: We both have to slave our guts out. So what's the odds?

SLATER: What you've got to show for it! That's the odds. Remember before the war? Wasn't our basic wage always more than yours? Isn't that proof positive? Once a slater always a slater! If you was to ask me today to lay tiles, I'd . . . why, even my youngest kid would kill himself laughing at the idea. I've got my professional pride: nobody can touch that! Not even a revolution!

Both pay and go out quarrelling.

TILER: You snob slater!

SLATER: Oh, go and lay tiles!

TILER: Very well, your lordship!

SLATER: Jealous! Jealous! That's all you are!

MAX: 'Workers of the world, unite!' 'The enlightened proletariat recognises no class distinctions'—and I don't think!

Notices HINKEMANN *who has just come in and sat down at a vacant table.*

Adam, what are you doing here?

HINKEMANN: *in a hoarse, jerky voice*] I was dry. I had a taste in my mouth—like animals' blood . . . sickening taste . . . like poison tearing at my throat . . . I had to have a drink . . . Christ, I'm no teetotaller, you don't have to stare at me like that!

MAX: Stare? Who, me? Why should I? I never need to wait for a nasty taste in my mouth before I head for the boozer. One look round the door of our kitchen at home—kitchen, drawing-room, dining-room, bathroom and nursery all rolled in one . . . one look at the poor kids . . . the thought of the wife nagging, nagging . . . and I about turn on the landing and seek salvation . . . in the boozer! I know . . . us husbands have a lot to answer for. Up to us to break the ice. At meetings we're ready to talk to total strangers about the great new life that's about to dawn and all that . . . at home we've just nothing to say to our wives.

While MAX is talking MICHAEL has come in. Hearing the last words he begins talking as soon as he's inside the door.

MICHAEL: Yes, happiness. You know where happiness dwells these days? In the mansions and great homes of the rich. Twenty rooms apiece and still too small. But the war has shaken the foundations. Even now they see the writing on the wall. Even now they feel the earth quaking beneath their feet. They are shaking in their shoes, for their hearts are black but their faces are pale, and their teeth are chattering with fright. Comrades, at last the day is dawning!

SEBALDUS: Your light is not the true light. Your light is as a pale flicker before the gates of the heavenly citadel. You seem to think that workers must all be party members. Many look to a different source altogether. That's what you always forget.

HINKEMANN: What about happiness, Comrade Michael? I've been doing a lot of thinking lately about what real happiness is. And . . . you know . . . I've come to the conclusion, that we can't bring *everybody* happiness . . . Real happiness, I think . . . is . . . [*breathing heavily*] something you've either got or you haven't got.

MICHAEL: Don't be so bourgeois, comrade. You make me laugh. [*With the rhetoric of the public speaker*] Out of the womb of historical developments in human conditions the new social structure is about to be born. Just as the sea eats away more and more of the coastline unobtrusively, so too we'll have developed unobtrusively into a socialist state. This is no fairy-tale! This is scientific fact! . . . Everything will follow the decrees of the party. It's all very simple. Happiness is inevitable. Instead of producing silks and satins because some lazy bitch wants silks and satins we start with cheap woollen clothing so that those who have nothing at all can be warmly dressed. Hence rationalised living conditions are created. It can all be summed up easily: rational humanity . . . And rational humanity produces happiness. Humanity thereby makes a mighty leap from the realm of want to the realm of freedom. Don't you see how simple it is?

[*Turning to* MAX] But people who believe they can skip the intermediate stages in the inevitable dialectic of history—anarchists and exotic dreamers who prefer faith to scientific fact . . .

MAX: . . . will be excommunicated, I know, I know. You've got your dogma! All you need now, old man, is the dog-collar. But you're wrong. The people don't need dogma, they need the will to revolution. If they haven't got that all your 'social conditions' won't help! And if the people *have* got the will to revolution then the New Life can begin whatever the conditions. Right now. This very day. No need to wait till the 'conditions' are right. But we know you lot! Take orders: yes. Take responsibility: no. Even when by your own lights 'conditions' have been ripe for action you've always flopped.

SEBALDUS: Neither is your light the true light, brother Max. My eyes have been opened, comrades. I have seen the light, the heavenly light and my feet are set on the straight and narrow path towards it.

PETER: It's all the same to me as long as I have peace and quiet . . . if anyone interferes with that . . . trouble!

MICHAEL: You're not a member of any party, Max. You're an anarchist . . . anybody not a party-member is free to say any irresponsible thing he likes. It's not worth while arguing with you. At least till you've joined a party. As for you, Sebaldus, you haven't seen the light, you're not even class-conscious yet. I'll say it once more. Social Conditions! All very simple.

HINKEMANN: *answers* MICHAEL] Maybe it is. Much of what you say is right . . . just what I've always thought . . . that business about silks and satins or warm clothing . . . man is no good when he's starving . . . he's got to have a roof over his head, something to eat and a little bit of beauty before you can expect him to be good . . . Maybe I'm a bit too slow on the uptake to grasp everything, see it all clearly, understand things properly, like you . . . you're a party official and you pick things up quicker . . . [MICHAEL *feels he is being got at and makes a gesture of annoyance so* HINKEMANN *hurriedly continues*] Not that I'm saying anything against the party. The party means an awful lot more to the worker than it does to the middle classes. For the middle classes a political party is just a political party. For the worker, well . . . he knows there are smudges . . . he knows there are smears in it . . . still for him the party *means* more. He puts all his belief in humanity, all his faith into the party . . . But . . . tell me something . . . suppose a man is sick . . . incurable . . . something wrong with him inside . . . or outside for that matter . . . incurable . . . can reasonable living conditions make that man happy?

MICHAEL: I don't quite see what you're getting at.

HINKEMANN: Yes, I often think myself I'm a bit muddled in the head since I was wounded in the war . . . Every morning when I get up I have to make an enormous effort to find the words or the ideas to make some kind of order out of the chaos that's inside me or surrounding me, touching me, fingering me, waiting to drown me . . . swamp me . . . Life is so strange . . . There's so much crowding in on you that you can't understand, can't grasp, things that make you scared . . . you can't see any sense in it . . . It makes you wonder if you can ever grasp Life at all . . . you begin to wonder if it's not like trying to empty the ocean with a teaspoon . . . trying to understand yourself . . . I mean you can't do it, can you? . . . All you can do is go on living, but when you look back on your life it's different and not like you lived it at all . . . you say to yourself sometimes, you're just a part of life to be lived and that's all there is to it . . . anybody who tries to get to the bottom of things and look for 'Truth' or even 'Purpose' is on the wrong track, like somebody looking for the 'Truth' or 'Purpose' of a cherry tree . . . By the time I've got myself out of that mess . . . well, when you get up in the morning there's chaos inside you and when you go to bed at night there's chaos inside you again . . . It's like it was before the Creation . . . So . . . well, I'll try to word my question better . . . take the men that got smashed up in the war. What's to become of them?

MICHAEL: Naturally society will see to it that they are properly fed and clothed and there's no reason why their life can't be just as happy as anybody else's.

HINKEMANN: What about somebody who has no arms?

MICHAEL: He'll be given artificial arms. Light work of some kind will be found for him if he's capable of it.

HINKEMANN: And what about somebody who has no legs?

MICHAEL: Society will look after him just the same as it will the man with no arms.

HINKEMANN: And what about the soul? What if there's something the matter there?

MICHAEL: *with robust lack of sentimentality*] Then he'd land in an asylum. But mind you, not the sort of asylum where people are treated like dumb animals. The mentally ill will have lots of loving care, they will be well treated, they will be treated like human beings.

HINKEMANN: I'm not thinking of people who are not right in the head or whose brains have been damaged . . . I'm thinking of people who are healthy enough physically and yet sick in their soul.

MICHAEL: There are no such people! People with healthy bodies have healthy souls. Why, it stands to reason. Either that or they're not right in the head and then they belong in an asylum.

HINKEMANN: Then there's another thing I wanted to ask. What if . . . during the war . . . somebody . . . [*he gulps*] . . . for instance . . . had his sex shot off . . . what . . . what would be done for him in the new society?

PETER *sniggers quietly.*

MICHAEL: *mopping his brow with a handkerchief*] You can certainly set some puzzlers! Makes me go hot under the collar . . . Nothing to laugh at, comrade Peter. That kind of thing can happen.

MAX: Makes you weep, not laugh.

SEBALDUS: The light of heaven would be bound to come to him out of God's infinite grace.

MICHAEL: Well, if I'm to answer that question . . . yes, if I'm to answer that question . . . as far as I know dialectical materialism has not considered that problem yet . . . Oh, what a fool I am! Hahaha! I do know the answer. There won't be any wars under the socialist society of the future! It's all perfectly simple.

HINKEMANN: Not so simple as all that. When the new society is set up some such cripples may already exist. How are they going to be happy? Or a man might have an accident at work . . . or anywhere . . . and lose his sex. How will he ever be happy?

MICHAEL: There you go again. That's a helluva difficult question.

MAX: Such subtleties! Man is better off not thinking about things like that. Soldiers of the Revolution like us don't need to worry about such subtleties. The people that kind of thing happens to are casualties, that's all. You have to allow for casualties in the Movement.

HINKEMANN: That's what I say too. But that's no reason why we can't talk about these things. I mean it does happen in life. And as we're on the subject anyway, I'll tell you the answer. I'll tell you a story . . . you see there was this man. Nobody special. Not a party leader or anything. Just rank and file. A worker . . . He was a friend of mine. I thought a lot of him. He got married when he was twenty. He'd met his wife at the works. They were a fine couple. It was always a joy to see them together. She was a fragile little thing, he was a man of steel . . . maybe even stronger than me . . . and was he proud of his strength . . . When the 'Heroes' War' broke out he was called up. Infantry. He hadn't any kids. Wasn't earning enough for that. He'd always thought a lot of his wife, naturally. But it wasn't till he got out there in the trenches that he thought he saw her as she really was. So good . . . so sweet . . . made him feel good just to think about her. He thought about her all the time. And gradually one big wish grew and grew inside him. A child! No, two . . . three . . . four . . . five children! Boys! Girls! What a wonderful mother she'd make. He'd forgotten what having a lot of children in a poor working class family was really like. What did the likes of us know about life, nature, the earth, the trees! We slaved like serfs all week. And on Sundays we'd go to some musty old movie and see a pack of lies. The lord of the manor rescuing some poor girl from the streets and the two of them living happily ever after. Crap like that. Christ, what a way to live! That was no life! That wasn't the real thing at all. A mechanical existence! . . . Anyway, one day in action he stopped a bullet. A nice little ticket home, he thought, and he was pretty happy. You see, he'd never been home on leave. When he came to in the hospital he started feeling his body. He felt a dressing round his groin. Aha, he thought, shot in the guts. Then he heard a voice from the next bed: 'Hello, our eunuch is coming to already. He's in for a shock when he sees what they've done to him'? And he thought to himself, they can't be talking about me surely. What do they mean, eunuch? And he went quite rigid. Shut his eyes again quickly. The way you shut out something horrible. He didn't sleep all night. Next morning they told him. At first he screamed and screamed for days on end . . . like a stuck pig . . . But then suddenly he noticed that his voice was a high-pitched screech. So he shut up again. He tried to think about his wife. But whenever he did he found he had to close his eyes at once and lie down rigid, as if he was unconscious, just like he had done the day after the operation . . . He wanted to hang himself. But he didn't have the nerve . . . So he was sent home. He came to my place first. We were good friends. What should he do? How was he to break it to his wife? He gave me the creeps. Well, well, I thought, so you're a . . . I was sorry for him, but all the same you couldn't help feeling a bit queer about him. When I thought about it, his position was a bit . . . well, funny. I didn't know what to say to him. Later I used to keep an eye on him. And his wife. I saw how much he was suffering. But how can you really see what's going on inside somebody? There you sit and here I sit. I see you. *How* do I see you? A few gestures, that's all I see, hear a few words. That's all . . . What do we really know or see of each other? . . . Nothing. Nothing.

He explodes.

He must have gone through sheer hell! He must have bled and bled! and bled! . . . It's a miracle he managed to go on living . . . Then one day he came to see me and you couldn't help seeing at once how much lovelier he looked. You can't really say that about a man, that he looked lovelier, I mean, but he did. You got the feeling he was a different person, somebody rich, somebody happy. And why? His wife didn't despise him, his wife didn't hate him, his wife didn't laugh at him . . . she could do anything she pleased, after all she was a healthy woman and he was a cripple . . . But he knew that in spite of everything . . . she loved him. You'd hardly believe it was possible . . . but that woman . . . how shall I put it . . . that woman loved . . . his soul.

Silence.

PAUL *comes in obviously intoxicated.*

PAUL: Evening all! Helluva quiet lot you are! Music! Music!

PAUL *puts a coin in the juke-box which begins to hammer out a military march.* PAUL *sits down at* HINKEMANN'S *table.*

PAUL: Evening, Adam.

HINKEMANN: Hello, Paul.

PAUL: *with the slurred speech of a drunk*] Don't wonder Greta finished with you . . . you . . . haha . . . you German hero!

HINKEMANN: What do you mean?

PAUL: You, the Incarnation of German Manhood! Haha! Devours live rats and mice! Haha!

HINKEMANN: How do you know that? Not so loud . . . it's horrible what I'm doing. I can't *tell* you how horrible. I'd rather rip open my own veins with my teeth. Some things should never be allowed. And this is one of them . . . You see, it's like this . . . Greta is not very well. The pension doesn't go very far. It's not my fault that we're out of work. But you see if a man can't even give his wife the basic necessities of life she's liable to turn against him. We don't want that. That's why . . . you won't tell Greta, will you, Paul? Promise, Paul, promise.

PAUL: I promise.

HINKEMANN: She's a funny girl, Greta, If she found out I was drinking rat's blood . . . I don't know . . . it would turn her stomach.

PAUL: *suddenly, with genuine indignation*] Listen . . . all this about the strongest man in the world, the hero of the German Empire— that's an out-and-out swindle. You'll have the police after you.

HINKEMANN: *suspiciously*] What are you getting at?

PAUL: What am I getting at? You know what I mean! You know why I promised not to tell Greta? Because she's seen you already.

HINKEMANN: *agitated*] What did she say? Did she cry? . . . Tell me . . . Tell me . . .

PAUL: Cry? What the hell is there to cry about? She laughed! It turned her stomach at first . . . then she laughed . . .

HINKEMANN: *going to pieces completely*] It turned her stomach at first, then she laughed . . . laughed . . . laughed . . . hahaha . . . she laughed . . .

PAUL: Well, it *is* a laugh, isn't it? He . . . he . . . haha . . . he makes himself out to be the strongest man in the world when he isn't a man at all! Not a man at all!

HINKEMANN: *suddenly very quiet*] Who . . . who told you that?

PAUL: Who? Greta.

HINKEMANN: When?

PAUL: At the show-ground.

HINKEMANN: How did you two come to be at the showground?

PAUL: Well . . . do you expect a young woman like that to live like a nun? How did we come to be there—what a question! You should be ashamed of yourself!

HINKEMANN: I should be? I should be ashamed of myself?

PAUL: Alright then, who should? Me? Greta? Who gives you the right to hang on to her anyway? She's got good grounds for divorce! Even the Catholic Church would allow that.

HINKEMANN: *calm, smiling bitterly*] You're right, I'd forgotten all about that. First my country sends me out to be shot to pieces. Then my wife has grounds for divorce because I'm no good any more. I'd forgotten that's the way of the world . . . And what are you going to do now . . . with Greta, I mean?

PAUL: None of your business.

HINKEMANN: You're right. It's really none of my business. Good grounds for divorce, that's all I am . . . But let's just suppose Greta was somebody else's wife and you're discussing her with a friend. What are you going to do?

PAUL: *pig-headedly*] Have some fun.

HINKEMANN: Greta's no slut . . . I think . . . can't we assume this is what will happen . . . The husband will let Greta go. Do you want to marry her?

PAUL: That's not what she's after at all. She just wants some fun too. The sooner you see that the better. And if she doesn't get enough fun with me, I'll send her on the streets . . . Then I'll be in clover.

HINKEMANN: *quietly, but with pent-up rage*] You . . . you filthy swine!

PAUL: Oh, I'm a filthy swine, am I? Do you really think I'd let her go on the streets! Call yourself my friend!

MAX: What's the matter with you two? Why pick on this place to have a fight? Why don't you take it out on your wives at home?

PAUL: We weren't fighting, we were just having a little joke.

MAX: If that was you having a joke I'd like to hear you having a fight.

PAUL: You see we went to the showground and . . .

HINKEMANN: *grabs hold of his arm*] Paul . . . don't say any more . . . never mind about me . . . it's Greta . . .

PAUL: . . . saw the Strongest Man in the World. A real bull of a man! Ate live rats and mice before your very eyes . . .

MAX: And Europeans call themselves civilised!

PAUL: And then I take a closer look at this fellow, and it's somebody I know. What a laugh! The Strongest Man in the World is a man I know who's had both his . . . [*gesture*] shot off. Bang, bang! . . . He wasn't a man any more, he was a bloody eunuch!

All present, including SEBALDUS *and* MICHAEL, *laugh uproariously.* HINKEMANN'S *wide, tortured eyes stare hypnotised by the laughter.*

PAUL: *shouting above the laughter*] That man was . . .

Just as he is about to say it, HINKEMANN *gets up. He stands in a pool of light. At first he speaks awkwardly, groping for words despite his passionate feelings; but in the end his speech has the overwhelming power of great simplicity.*

HINKEMANN: That man was Hinkemann! Go on, laugh! Laugh all of you! Just like she did! Don't stop! You've never seen a freak like me in your life before! A real live eunuch. Shall I give you a song?

Sings in a squeaky voice:

'Don't you cry, when we must part'

If you poke a canary's eyes out it'll sing . . . I'm almost as good . . . You fools! What do you know about how much a poor miserable creature can suffer? What a change there'd have to be in the whole lot of you, before you could build a better world! You fight the bloated bourgeoisie and you're just as bloated yourselves, just as superior and mean and selfish! You hate each other because each of you swears by a different party programme from the next fellow. Nobody trusts his neighbour. Squabbling and treachery smothers everything you do. You have words, fine words, wonderful holy words, about Eternal Happiness. They're only good for healthy people! You don't see where you fall short . . . there are some people no state, no society, no family, no community can ever bring happiness to. Our need starts where your cures leave off.

There man stands alone.

There the message of the bottomless pit is: no comfort.

There the message in the vault of heaven is: no happiness.

There the message of the green woods is: mockery and scorn.

There the message in the roaring of the sea is: ridicule.

There the message of the choking darkness is: no love.

There who brings help?

Silence for a few seconds. HINKEMANN *stumbles out of the door.*

MAX: Where are you going?

HINKEMANN: *his face distorted as if by a vision*] She laughed!

The following scene is played very quickly. The stage in semi-darkness. Only the silhouettes of the various people can be made out.

MICHAEL: *rushes out the door*] Hinkemann! Hinkemann! . . . Gone! . . . If I'd only guessed . . . This rotten world we live in is to blame!

SEBALDUS: *rapturously*] I have sinned against the light. I have seen a man crucified and laughed!

PAUL: *in a maudlin voice*] My God, We've got to do something for him . . .

PETER: You're a swine, you are, Paul . . . and no mistake!

MAX: *pushing back his chair in disgust*] All very simple! Who said that? Nothing is simple . . . How much do I owe you, Miss?

Curtain.

ACT III

Scene 1

The stage suggests: a street in the West End. Evening. The curtain rises on HINKEMANN *clinging to a lamp-post in the foreground. A little* BOY *comes up to him.*

BOY: Got a sister, just thirteen.

HINKEMANN: *absently*] Is that so?

BOY: She's lovely. Just thirteen.

HINKEMANN: *mechanically*] You hungry?

BOY: She's got a room to herself. Only just turned thirteen.

HINKEMANN buys hot dogs from a street vendor—an old woman. Gives them to the BOY.

HINKEMANN: So your sister's just thirteen . . . And how old are you?

BOY: Seven . . . [*starts to eat the hot dogs*] Thanks, mister. All the same—no use talking to you . . . slow in the uptake you are . . . you don't get the idea . . .

The little BOY runs off. The street lights go on. The street is busy. The SHOWMAN *comes on dressed in top-hat and tails, slightly inebriated.*

SHOWMAN: Just a minute! Aren't you . . . of course, it's Hinkemann. Hello, Hinkemann! You shouldn't be showing yourself in the street for all to see. Remember you're a rare bird. Have to pay for the pleasure of seeing a man like you. Star turn! Sweep the continent! Sensational discovery . . . Why are you staring like that? Look like a ghost.

HINKEMANN: Sir . . . Murder is on the loose again! Sir . . . look around you! Look around you! You know what has happened, sir? I too have eyes to see. I've had my eyes opened for me! What blinding light! Night! Let there be night! Let there be night!

SHOWMAN: Been in the boozer, I suppose? Powerful stuff hooch! Pin your ears back, Hinkemann! Listen to the voice of experience! A bottle of wine's better anytime than any amount of hooch! That stuff is good business for the barman but bad medicine for the customer.

HINKEMANN: No, no, sir. I wasn't wasting my time in there. They've opened my eyes for me. Now I can see! All the way! Right to the naked heart. I see what men are! I see the age we live in! Sir . . . the war's on again! Men are murdering each other and laughing! *Men are murdering each other and laughing!*

SHOWMAN: So now you can see, can you? In that case you must see that nobody's thinking about war. Put on a 'Horrors of War' show and you won't make a penny today. That's out! Competition is the pass-word in Europe these days! Double your money easy! It's hectic! Jazz! Jazz! Razzamatazz! Look about you, man. Top performance is what counts! Performance! That's the key to the age! Doesn't matter what in, as long as you make the top! Heavyweight champion of the world! Party Leader. Black market king! Six-day cycle racer! Film star! Evangelist! Solo tenor! Fascist! Nazi chief! Jew-baiter! Business is booming! You've got to ride the wave! You can be up to your neck in rottenness and still come out healthy. Morality? As much as you need given away free with every packet. [*Laughs*] Had some fun with a negress up in Hamburg once . . . they've got what it takes! . . . Well, see you tomorrow. Be on time!

HINKEMANN: No, sir. That's finished.

SHOWMAN: He's joking! Priceless! Just when you've got your hand in! Just when you can do it to a band playing.

Sings the 'British Grenadiers'.

'Of all the world's great heroes'
Crunch! You put your teeth into the first one! . . .
'There's none that can compare'
Ladies and Gentlemen; any blood-suckers among you? . . .
'With a tow row, row, row, row, row'
Come along, ladies and gentlemen, anybody like to try? Don't be bashful, don't be shy.
Alright, Homunculus! Go home and sleep it off!

HINKEMANN: Begging your pardon, sir . . . I can't come back . . . The advance you gave me . . . got to put everything right . . . can't have them saying I cheated people out of their money. Got to put everything right.

SHOWMAN: What? You mean it's no hangover? You're serious? No go, friend! A joke's a joke but this is business. You're under contract for the season, remember! [*Brutally*] I can use legal compulsion, boy. Force you to do the job. Bourgeois society is built on the idea of contract. You're violating everything the nation holds sacred. I've law and order behind me. Nothing doing, boy. Either you turn out tomorrow and on time or I'll have the police drag you there. [*Changing his tone*] Come on, Hinkemann, don't be difficult, it's for your own good. Just want to keep you out of prison.

HINKEMANN: Prison, sir? All the rats and mice I had to kill with my teeth—they were in prison before they went to the scaffold. And there are a lot of people at liberty who are really in prison though they have committed no crime—like beasts in a cage. A window with wire-mesh that lets no light through. Walls that choke out life. Chains that eat into your flesh. You can't scare me, sir. And anyway, sir [*screaming with hate*] you! . . . You and Satan! You're Satan himself. You feed people on blood! You strip people of shame! I . . . I . . . grrh . . . I . . . but there'll be other men, other men who'll! who'll!! . . . you don't know, do you, about the woman who laughed at Homunculus? My own wife! [*Savagely*] That was her last laugh. She's going to cry for a change. But . . . they're all deaf . . . they hear nothing . . . their ears are filled with laughter and ridicule.

SHOWMAN: *taken aback*] Well, I never! The man who stumbles about all the time as if he couldn't string three words together. And here he harangues with the best of them! . . . What have I done? Why pick on me? I'm a good solid citizen, just like any other business man . . . [*jovially*] Still . . . can't take you seriously, Hinkemann. You're drunk. Have it out with you tomorrow. Have fun, stay alive and kicking! A man just goes to the dogs if he can't have some action. Man with your gifts! . . . So long, my hit of the season. See you tomorrow.

SHOWMAN *goes off*.

192

HINKEMANN: *alone*] Tomorrow . . . the way he says that . . . tomorrow, as if there was bound to be a tomorrow. Oh, I see! I see! Oh! the light! Oh, my eyes . . . my eyes . . .

HINKEMANN *breaks down completely. From now on the scene must be like a nightmare* HINKEMANN *is having. The figures seem to crowd in upon him as they step out of the darkness and are swallowed up in it.*

From all sides one-armed, one-legged war veterans, with barrel-organs, converge concentrically. They are nonchalantly singing the following wartime song:

It's a long way to Tipperary! . . .

They stop suddenly. In rapid succession they shout one after the other:

This is *my* pitch!

Not one shows any readiness to give way to the others. They all shout together:

My pitch!

A few seconds' silence. Since no-one gives way, as at a word of command they all suddenly start to move singing and playing their barrel-organs, marching straight at each other. They fanatically turn the handles of their barrel-organs and sing the following song, as if they were inflamed with revolutionary ardour, and in the act of storming a right-wing reactionary barricade:

'Down with the dogs, down with the dogs,
Down with the dogs of the reactionary right'.

The barrel-organs meet with a great crash. Recoiling from the impact the men return to the assault. Police come running up. They shout:

'Law and order!'
'In the name of the Law!'
'Atten-shun!'

Sudden silence, as if long-familiar words of command were slowly getting through to the minds of the veterans. They do an about-turn. March round the stage smartly and off in various directions, each keeping to his own separate orbit, turning their barrel-organs and singing stoutly:

'It's a long way to Tipperaray' etc. etc.

Newspaper-boys run across the stage.

FIRST BOY: Extra! Extra! Sensational news! New night club opened! Strip-tease! Jazz! Champagne! American bar!

SECOND BOY: Extra! Extra! Latest sensation! Jews massacred in Galicia! Synagogue burned down! One thousand burnt to death!

A VOICE: Hurrah! Send them all to Galicia.

THIRD BOY: Trixy Try! Beautiful continental film star! Trixy plays lead in crime drama: 'The Sex Maniac and Her Forty Men!' Sensational! Brutal! Soul-stirring!

FOURTH BOY: Plague in Finland! Mothers drown own children! Eye-witness reports! Outbreaks of mob violence! Our Government sending troops to maintain law and order! One hundred tanks on the way!

FIFTH BOY: New spirit in Germany! Reawakening of moral sensibility! Our age under the sign of Christ! Stirring film drama: 'The Passion of Our Lord'. Famous actress Glin Glanda plays the saviour! Two-million dollar production. Also showing Dempsey-Carpentier fight.

SIXTH BOY: Greatest discovery of the Twentieth Century! Levicite! Technological miracle. Record-breaking poison-gas! One aircraft capable of annihilating any city in the world! Honorary degree for inventor! Pope confers title!

SEVENTH BOY: Dollar slump! Dollar Slump! Increased birth-rate expected! Latest calculations from the Bureau of Census. Responsible professors jubilant!

EIGHTH BOY: Stock Exchange open to all! Every man his own investor! Double your money! Poverty wiped out! Poverty wiped out!

Two old POLISH JEWS cross the stage.

FIRST JEW: It's the old story. They flogged us. They dragged us out of bed at dead of night, they took our women and girls . . . The hand of God has smitten us with suffering.

SECOND JEW: Suffering! We are the chosen people! Aren't we the chosen people! Chosen! Chosen for suffering! What a great gift he has bestowed upon us!

They go off.

A LITTLE LOVE MACHINE: He was so nice, just a kid . . . so I stayed all night . . . this was all he had to give me . . .

HER CASH REGISTER: Who do you think you are, the vicar's daughter, doing it for love! You'll get a mouthful of fist next time you try that . . .

LITTLE LOVE MACHINE: But you know I'm not well . . .

They go off.

OLD WOMAN SELLING HOT DOGS: Our Saviour is coming, sir. Do not deny him. He brings back hope to old women like me. The new dawn cometh. The Kingdom of Zion is nigh.

CUSTOMER: I bet you put all your savings into it too.

OLD WOMAN: Who cares, sir, who cares for filthy lucre. An old wreck like me can't be worse off. The tribulations of this world hold no terrors for me. I've drunk of them to the dregs. Oh, my soul thirsts for deliverance. I know that the Kingdom of Zion is nigh . . .

Moves on.
A STREET VENDOR *sidles up to a* STUFFED SHIRT *in a monocle.*

VENDOR: Latest remedy, sir, for vanishing virility—called 'Go-Man'.

STUFFED SHIRT WITH MONOCLE: I always use 'Togetherness'.

VENDOR: That's not made any more. Didn't sell. Poor in protein. We're selling it for boot polish.

They move on.

SHOUTS: Man on the ground!
He's in a fit!
Police!

VOICES: That's Homunculus from the showground. It's all that rat's blood. No wonder!

A RUBBER COSH: Probably a bloody Red . . . we'd have made short work of him in the old days . . . Put a gun in his hand . . . make the bastard blow his brains out . . . that or have his head bashed in with a rifle butt! Make them sing the national anthem first . . . hehehe! The scum has got to come to heel . . . needs a touch of the boot . . .

A FLAME THROWER: Our mob never took prisoners. Orders were: Into the nearest field with him . . . boot up the arse to make him run . . . a bang on the head . . . Standard formula afterwards: 'Prisoner shot while attempting to escape'.

PROSTITUTES *come running from all directions.*

FIRST PROSTITUTE: Homunculus can sleep with me. Take him to my place. I'll give him a glass of wine, he'll come round.

SECOND PROSTITUTE: No . . . take him to my place!

THIRD PROSTITUTE: To mine! To mine!

FOURTH PROSTITUTE: You old whore! Where do you come in! Haven't even got your discharge from hospital! Beat it!

THIRD *and* FOURTH PROSTITUTES *begin fighting. Blast of martial music from the next street. Fife and drums. Then full military band.*

SCREECH: Soldiers! Soldiers! Hip! Hip! Hurrah!

All rush off: HINKEMANN *is left alone. The street is empty. Even the street lights fade and grow dark at the sound of the band. The music fades into the distance.* HINKEMANN *gets up.*

HINKEMANN: Boundless heavens above me . . .

Eternal stars above me . . .

The stage darkens.

Scene 2

The stage suggests: HINKEMANN'S *home.* MAX *stands by the table waiting.* HINKEMANN *comes in carrying something wrapped in a parcel. His eyes have a feverish gleam and his movements have a new jumpy quality.*

MAX: I've been waiting for you, Hinkemann . . . I wanted to give my reasons . . .

HINKEMANN: No need, friend. Reasons are not good enough. Feelings are the real test . . . Know what I've got in my hand?

MAX: No idea.

HINKEMANN: *The* root of the matter! *The* root! I happened to look in a shop window and I couldn't believe my eyes. I didn't know whether to laugh or cry. I close my eyes. I think I must be dreaming. But no, when I open them again it's still there in the window. I go out into the shop and ask why they put it there. That's a Priapus, says the salesman. When he sees I don't understand he explains how the ancient Greeks and Romans

196

used to worship him as a god. The women, you mean? I ask.
No, men and women both, he replies. I ask if it's for sale. Yes.
On instalments? They don't do business that way. Sorry, I say,
the working man is so used to it. I left my watch and took the god.

HINKEMANN *has taken a little bronze Priapus out of its wrapping.*
Places it on the mantelpiece. Lights a candle beside it.

MAX: *coaxingly*] You aren't feeling well, Hinkemann . . . I can
see . . . you're not yourself . . .

HINKEMANN: Quite well.

MAX: You know . . . I think . . . I'll just stay with you till
your wife comes.

HINKEMANN: Two's company . . . three's a crowd.

MAX: How d'you mean?

HINKEMANN: I'll tell you. Do you ever really see people in the street?

MAX: You certainly ask some funny questions.

HINKEMANN: You walk along the streets, day after day, like a
blind man. And then all of a sudden you *see*. Max, what you see
is terrible. You see souls. And do you know what souls look
like? Not like any living thing. One soul is a bull-neck, the
next a love-machine, the third a cash-register, the fourth a
soldiers' organisation, the fifth a rubber cosh . . . Did you
ever poke a little bird's eyes out? [*Without waiting for an answer*]
The sins of the mothers shall be visited upon the children unto
the fourth generation. Isn't that what the Good Book says? . . .
Good night, Max. No offence . . . I know . . . I know . . . you
had your reasons . . . I've found *the* root of the matter . . .

MAX: I'd better stay.

HINKEMANN: Go . . . go . . . Greta'll be here in a minute . . .
What you heard in the pub was just the drink talking . . .

MAX: Oh, well . . . good night, Hinkemann.

HINKEMANN: Good night, Max . . . Just one thing more. How
long have you been married?

MAX: Twenty-three years.

HINKEMANN: You did think about a divorce once, didn't you?

MAX: I did once. But we've got sort of used to each other. What
keeps us together is the children.

HINKEMANN: What keeps you together—the children, of course
. . . They call divorce 'separation from bed and board', don't they?

MAX: That's what they call it.

HINKEMANN: And your wife's religious, isn't she?

MAX: Never misses mass . . . What's a man to do? As far as I'm concerned she can go to church if she gets a kick out of it . . . [*At the door*] Good night.

MAX goes out. HINKEMANN alone.

HINKEMANN: They have no other Gods but thee. They lie to themselves, deceive themselves, try to make themselves believe they are worshipping the Crucified Christ. All the time they're praying to thee. All their Hail Mary's rise to thee, all their Our Father's make a rosary round thy nakedness, all their processions a dance in thine honour. Thou wearest no mask, thou dost not shroud thyself in lying words. Thou art Alpha and Omega, the beginning and the end. Thou art the truth, thou art the God of all peoples . . . Thou hast cast out thy servant, O my God, but thy servant raises up an altar to thee . . . Ah, I do believe he is laughing! Go on, laugh, that's right, laugh! Men laughed at me and had no cause to laugh. Now it's your turn to laugh . . . for ever and ever! You have a right to laugh.

Noise on the stairs.

HINKEMANN: That will be Greta now . . . Dark night is coming and my eyes are going blind.

OLD MRS. HINKEMANN comes in.

OLD MRS. HINKEMANN: Good evening.

HINKEMANN: Oh—it's you! Good evening, mother. What brings you here at this time of night? Since when have you been going out at night? Warm summer night tempt you out? . . . The swallows were flying low today. There's going to be a storm.

OLD MRS. HINKEMANN: He's come back.

HINKEMANN: Who?

OLD MRS. HINKEMANN: Father.

HINKEMANN: Whose father?

OLD MRS. HINKEMANN: Your father.

HINKEMANN: Mother, what are you talking about? My father died when I was only six months old. You've told me yourself again and again!

OLD MRS. HINKEMANN: I told you lies. He *was* dead. As far as I was concerned he was dead. You were only six months old. Still

198

at this breast, so withered now. Then one night he came home. Drunk. Arm in arm with a woman. One he'd picked up in the street. He shouted at me: 'Wife!' he shouted. 'Go home to your mother and sleep there. My bed needs warm young blood. You give me the shivers since you had that brat' . . . I just stood there and stared at him. And suddenly . . . it wasn't my husband standing there before me eyes, but an animal, a strange animal come to tear me to pieces and take away my child. I went for him with a carving-knife . . . He just roared with laughter and went off with this woman. He didn't come back that night. Nor the next. He just abandoned me as if he'd never known of my existence. I went on the streets . . . to make enough to feed you. I wasn't bad-looking when I was young. And today . . .

HINKEMANN: Today?

OLD MRS. HINKEMANN: He came back. Dressed in rags, filthy clothes on his lousy body. Bloated, sick and shaking, that's how he came into the room. I knew his step on the stairs. 'What do you want with me after twenty-nine years?' I asked him. And this evil old man mumbled like an idiot: 'You won't beat me, will you?' And then: 'I've come home to die'.

HINKEMANN: And what did you say to him, mother?

OLD MRS. HINKEMANN: I told him to take his clothes off and get into bed. I told him he'd find clean underwear in the dresser, hot water on the stove and soap in the drawer.

HINKEMANN: Then you've forgiven him, mother?

OLD MRS. HINKEMANN: *harshly*] No, and I'll never forgive him. I'll look after him till he dies. I'm a human being and I'll do my duty. When he dies, I'll close his eyes, that's no job for a stranger . . . But when the hearse comes for him to take him to the cemetery, then I'll pull down the blinds and lock the doors and I will not walk behind his coffin. [*Triumphantly*] Leave him to be buried by strangers! That'll be my revenge for what he's done to me!

HINKEMANN: *after a pause*] What was it hurt most, mother? Having to starve while he drank his wages?

OLD MRS. HINKEMANN: No.

HINKEMANN: Him bringing home a woman off the streets?

OLD MRS. HINKEMANN: No.

HINKEMANN: Was it because he wanted to sleep with her in your bed?

OLD MRS. HINKEMANN: No.

HINKEMANN: Then it was because he just laughed when your tortured soul revolted.

OLD MRS. HINKEMANN: Yes, my son, that was it.

HINKEMANN: Then you are doing the right thing, mother. I don't want to see my father and, like you, I will not walk behind his coffin.

Silence.

OLD MRS. HINKEMANN: I . . . I need a suit for your father.

HINKEMANN: Here, he can have my Sunday best.

Takes a suit from the wardrobe. Gives it to OLD MRS. HINKEMANN.

OLD MRS. HINKEMANN: It should fit him . . . you know, your father was always very particular about his clothes . . . Is Greta in?

HINKEMANN: She'll be back soon . . . Mother, you've got your cross to bear and I've got mine. But at least you can talk about yours . . . it's different for me, I can't say a word to anybody for fear they'd just roar with laughter at me.

OLD MRS. HINKEMANN: Everybody has his cross to bear. Nobody is spared. Life is too much for us. I must be getting back. Father'll be getting hungry. Good night.

HINKEMANN: Good night, mother.

OLD MRS. HINKEMANN *goes out.*

HINKEMANN: That was what hurt most. Laughing at her when her poor soul writhed in suffering, raw with pain. Didst thou hear, oh mighty God? Art thou content? Two human sacrifices offered up to thee . . . My father the brave knight who champions women of the street, my mother a cooing little love bird. Shall we do a dance of joy before thee? To hear is to obey! I am capable of anything! Drink rats' blood for a few coppers, dance for two human lives.

HINKEMANN *begins to perform a loose-jointed dance in front of the Priapus. The tempo is slow at first but soon develops into a wild and violent rhythm with* HINKEMANN *leaping from one leg to the other.*

HINKEMANN: It's a scream! a scream!

Hip, hip, hurrah!

Step this way, ladies and gentlemen!

Have your tickets ready!

The more the merrier!

Ho ho ho! Ho ho ho!

HINKEMANN *drops onto a stool. After a moment* FRANKIE *comes in.*

FRANKIE: Hullo, Greta not here?

HINKEMANN: No.

FRANKIE: You don't half look sad, sitting there . . . There's something in the air on a warm summer's night . . . I'm going dancing . . . Like to come along?

HINKEMANN: You, you! Oh! Sorry . . . I was thinking about something else . . .

FRANKIE: Listen, Adam . . .

HINKEMANN: Yes.

FRANKIE: Listen, Adam . . .

HINKEMANN: Go on!

FRANKIE: You're still a fine upstanding fellow . . . the best-looking of the whole bunch . . .

HINKEMANN: Well?

FRANKIE: Well, I was just thinking . . .

HINKEMANN: Yes?

FRANKIE: Well, when you hear what Greta's like these days . . . all moody . . . she's my best friend, and I don't want to say anything, but, well, I don't envy you . . . [*Close up to* HINKE-MANN] Come on Adam . . . why don't you come with me . . . You can tell Greta the Party called a branch meeting . . . why don't you see what I'm getting at!

HINKEMANN: I see . . . you mean, why don't we spend the night together? That what you're driving at? The night is warm. Cats courting on every landing. Down in Civic Park there's . . . something in the air . . .

FRANKIE: It's warm enough to sleep on a bench in the park . . . oh, Adam . . .

FRANKIE *twines herself round him, kisses him.* HINKEMANN *pushes her away, gives a shout of laughter.*

FRANKIE: *furiously*] Do you think I'm chasing you?

HINKEMANN: Go chase yourself. There are plenty of men in the park. Tom-cats, she-cats, dogs and bitches. It's in the air.

FRANKIE: *snarling*] Just wait. I'll get my own back!

FRANKIE *runs out.*

HINKEMANN: Hahaha! Hinkemann is not dead, he is a God! There's a naked bronze God in the market-place. They buzz round like

bees round honey! . . . Walk up, walk up, ladies and gentlemen!
You will be amazed! . . . And they say I'm grounds for divorce!

A few seconds' silence. GRETA *comes in.*

GRETA: Hullo, Adam.

HINKEMANN: *without looking up*] And the Lord said unto Cain:
Where is thy brother Abel? And he answered: Am I my
brother's keeper?

GRETA: It's me, Adam.

HINKEMANN: But the Lord said: Thy brother's blood cries to
heaven for vengeance.

GRETA: I've brought you some flowers, Adam . . . Today is our
wedding anniversary . . .

HINKEMANN: Some people have a kind of mask, they can be
laughing at you and be all over you all in the same breath . . .
Thanks, Greta. It's good of you. Asters are bright, aren't they!
Does you good to look at the colours! Our wedding day was
lovely . . . and our wedding night . . . was lovely too.

GRETA: It was peace-time.

HINKEMANN: Yes, and then came the war. You said: You're in
the Guards, I'm so proud of you. And when I left for the front
you cried. Were you crying for joy because I was in the Guards?

GRETA: We had such great hopes for the future!

HINKEMANN: Yes, the future looked as bright as these flowers.
But you know, when there were asters growing anywhere during
the war, a shell would drop on them and things weren't so
bright any more. Plants and animals, animals and people . . .
it's all the same. I was a strapping fellow in those days, living
life to the full without thinking twice about it. You used to be
jealous in those days.

GRETA: Yes.

HINKEMANN: *harshly*] No need for you to be jealous any more,
nowadays you can just . . . laugh!

GRETA: *begins to cry*]

HINKEMANN: Go on, laugh! Crying? Don't put on an act! Laugh,
woman, laugh! Laugh like you know how. You laugh when
you see a man lay down his scarred and naked soul in the filth
of the street. Spare your tears! Ah, I know . . . you want a
song first! [*Sings shrilly the opening strains of the Merry Widow*

202

Waltz] Why don't you laugh? [*Exhausted*] I pressed the right button, didn't I?

GRETA: *with outstretched palms and fingers spread in terror as if expecting to be attacked*] You're staring at me so strangely . . . I'm scared of you.

HINKEMANN: Scared? Nonsense! How can you be scared of me . . . when I haven't even got . . . haven't even got . . .

GRETA: *Quickly, humbly*] No, no, I'm not really scared. I love you, how could I be scared?

HINKEMANN: Tell the truth, woman!

GRETA: I want to.

HINKEMANN: I know the whole story.

GRETA: I've been bad, Adam.

HINKEMANN: You're not telling lies?

GRETA: I've been bad. I'm a weak woman. It just came over me. I loved you and at the same time I didn't love you. It wasn't right of me—I don't know if you can ever care for me again.

HINKEMANN: I can't blame you for going with Paul. You're quite entitled to if you're in love with him.

GRETA: *failing to understand*] Then you don't love me?

HINKEMANN: *Because* I love you.

GRETA: *still failing to understand*] No . . . no . . .

HINKEMANN: But you must go away, Greta, at once! . . . Or, no . . . I'll go . . . I've got no claims. The furniture is yours. Good-bye.

GRETA: Adam! Oh, my dear! . . . My poor dear husband! I've betrayed you for thirty pieces of silver . . . I've treated you badly, I've been the lowest of the low!

HINKEMANN: Woman! . . . Woman! . . . Where have you been the last few weeks to learn to lie like that? Or have I been deaf all along? Did I never know who I had right here inside my own four walls? Has the whole world turned topsy turvy? The butterfly I thought I was sheltering turned into a worm! A worm with eyes as false as a poor whore who has to put on an act just to make a living. [*In wild rage*] Don't touch me! Let go my hands! Maybe my shot-up body made you sick, but now, woman, you make me sick! Your hands: toads, sickening and slimy! Your breasts, your round, firm little breasts: like rotten filth! Your mouth, your sweet, red mouth:

a stinking cesspool! Your body, your healthy body, your strong, healthy, flowering body . . . I loathe the sight of it! Rotting with corruption for all its health! Nothing but a dead carcass in my sight!

GRETA: *on her knees*] Lash me with your tongue! . . . lash me! . . . beat me! . . . beat me! . . . It's what I deserve!

HINKEMANN: How could you stand there at the fair-ground and listen to your own husband being put on show like a wild beast . . . see your own husband take innocent creatures and tear open their throats with his teeth . . . to earn money for you! Rip open the throats of live animals! . . . You stood there with your lover and . . . laughed! laughed!

GRETA: That's not true . . . Before God, that's not true.

HINKEMANN: I can't bear to talk to you. You're lying . . . not like a human being. You're lying with the cunning of a devil. Good-bye!

HINKEMANN *turns to go.*

GRETA: Adam, say anything, anything you like . . . but don't go . . . I accept the blame for all the wrong that has been done . . . yes, I laughed at the showground . . . I laughed . . . like this: hahahaha! . . .

HINKEMANN: And for that you must die, woman. Not for taking another man—you had a right to . . . not for lying to me— you thought you had a right to . . . you must die, because you laughed at me at the showground. A mother can strangle her child and no-one need cast a stone at her. But if she were to strangle her child and then laugh at the sight of the baby's swollen tongue sticking out of its throat . . . then she should burn in hell to all eternity! I'll let you off lightly, woman. I won't let you suffer till the end of time . . . What are you on your knees in front of me for? Kneel to *him* . . . He is your god. Pray to him! . . . Pray!

HINKEMANN *drags* GRETA *to the image of Priapus. His breathing has turned to a moan.*

HINKEMANN: *after a few seconds*] Why . . . why are you staring at me like that? What's that look in your eyes? . . . As I'm human there's no lie in your eyes! . . . I know these eyes! . . . I've seen these eyes in the factory . . . I've seen these eyes in the barracks . . . I've seen these eyes in the hospital . . . I've seen these eyes in prison. The same eyes. The eyes of the hunted, beaten, tortured, tormented creature . . . Yes, Greta, I thought you had so much more than me, and it turns out you're just as miserable and helpless as I am . . . Well, if that's the way it is . . . then we're brother and sister I am you and you are me . . . So what's to become of us?

GRETA: I will never leave you again.

HINKEMANN: That's not what I mean, Greta. That's all over and done with. What does it matter to us? What does it matter if you go with another man, what does it matter if you tell me lies, what does it matter if you laugh at me. It doesn't do you any good. Even if you were to dress like a fine lady and live in a grand house and never stop laughing—all the same, you're still nothing but a poor unhappy creature just like me. I have only just realised that . . . Leave me alone, Greta . . .

GRETA: Leave you alone, now?

HINKEMANN: You must leave me alone, always. And I must leave you alone, always.

GRETA: What's to become of us?

HINKEMANN: Once, about six years ago, I was in a bad way. I was starving and my mouth would water at the very sight of somebody eating! You've no idea what it felt like, Greta, to walk across the children's playgrounds in the better parts of town and see some little kid take a great big happy bite out of a juicy sandwich! The greed that comes over you! Then all of a sudden the pangs of hunger are gone! You just feel mad at the kid doing the chewing! You're ready to commit murder just so you won't have to see him chewing any more!

GRETA: What does all this mean, Adam? I don't see the point.

HINKEMANN: It's my own fault if I get laughed at. I should have been doing something about it back in the days when the real criminals, the politicians and generals were just beginning the work of bringing the world down in flames about our ears. I did nothing. I am as ridiculous as the age we live in, as sadly ridiculous as our own age. Our age has no soul. I have no sex. Where's the difference. Let's each go our own way. You yours. I mine.

GRETA: What does all this mean, Adam?

HINKEMANN: Just this: I've seen and understood, but I don't know how long it will last. The force of nature in a man is stronger than his reason. Reason can be a source of self-deception.

GRETA: And what's to become of me?

HINKEMANN: You're strong and healthy. The way things are there's no place for a cripple in this world . . . you have to be of some *use* or you're no good. Either a man's healthy, in which case his soul is healthy. This is the voice of good healthy common sense. Or a man's mentally sick, in which case he ought to be put away. It's not quite like that, but it's not all that wrong either. A man who is sick can't do anything, it's like a lark with dead wings, like a captive eagle with its sinews cut . . . Goodbye, Greta. I wish you a happy life.

GRETA: What are you going to do . . . what are you going to do . . . You won't leave me alone? . . .

HINKEMANN: It's not because of my sickness . . . It's not because my body is shot to pieces . . . I walked through the streets, I saw no human beings . . . masks, nothing but grinning masks. On my way home I saw masks, nothing but grinning masks . . . and suffering . . . blind creature-suffering, senseless and endless . . . I haven't enough strength left. Enough strength to fight, enough strength to dream. A man who hasn't the strength left to dream hasn't the strength left to live. My bullet was a fruit from the tree of the knowledge of good and evil . . . For me, all seeing becomes knowing, and all knowing suffering . . . Then all suffering turned into: will . . . the will to suffer no more.

GRETA: You're going to kill yourself! . . . Adam . . . Adam . . . I *didn't* laugh! Adam! Listen to me! I *didn't* laugh! Listen, my dear . . . I'll stay with you. For ever and ever! Everything's going to be all right again. Just the two of us. We'll be so close for warmth. You beside me. Me beside you.

HINKEMANN: You didn't laugh . . . look at me, Greta . . . I believe you, Greta . . . darling [*kisses her tenderly*] Everything's going to be all right again . . . Just the two of us.

GRETA: *clinging to him*] Summertime and silence in the forest . . . Stars above and walking hand in hand.

HINKEMANN: *breaking away from her*] Autumn and the green leaves wither. Stars . . . and hatred! . . . fist raised against fist . . .

GRETA: *screams*] Adam!

HINKEMANN: *tiredly*] I know too much.

GRETA: *weeping helplessly like a child*] Don't leave me alone . . . I
get lost in the dark . . . I hurt myself . . . I fall . . . I'm all
raw flesh . . . How it hurts! How it hurts! . . . Oh . . .
Oh . . . I'm so afraid of life! Imagine! All alone! All alone
in life! Alone in a jungle of hunted animals! . . . No good
people left these days. They all tear at your heart . . . Don't
leave me alone!! Don't leave me alone!!! God has his chosen
path for me. I belong with you.

HINKEMANN: What is against Nature cannot be God's will.—Try,
Greta, try . . . you do the fighting . . . you are healthy . . .
start a new life . . . fight for a better world . . . a world for
the likes of us . . .

GRETA: *her shoulder twitching*] Even if . . . even if I wanted to . . .
I just can't go on . . . I haven't any fight left in me. My spirit
is broken [*In desperation*] Oh God, I'll never find my way out.
We're caught, Adam, caught in a spider's web. There's a spider
sitting in the centre that won't let us go. It's spun its mesh
tight around us. I can scarcely move my head. I don't understand
what life's about any more . . . and deliver us from evil, Jesus
Christ my saviour . . .

Goes out with heavy step.

HINKEMANN: *alone*] Where does it start and where does it finish?
How can you tell with a spider's web? [HINKEMANN *seizes the
Priapus and flings it into the fireplace*]

HINKEMANN: You lying God! You poor miserable wretch! . . .
[*After a pause*] If that's how things are who has the right to judge
his neighbour? We are all condemned to judge ourselves . . .
Deliverance! Deliverance! In all the streets in the world they
cry for deliverance! The Frenchman who fired the bullet that
crippled me, the negro who fired the bullet that crippled me
is maybe crying for deliverance. Wonder if he's still alive?
Wonder what *his* life is like? . . . Is he blind, wanting an arm,
or a leg? He got me and somebody else got him . . . But who
got all of us? . . . We are *one* spirit, *one* flesh. To think there
are people in the world who can't see that. And people who've
forgotten it. The war was the same for all of them, they suffered

hardships and hated their officers and obeyed orders and killed each other! . . . All forgotten . . . It will be the same next time, they'll suffer hardships, and hate their officers again and then . . . they'll obey orders and . . . kill each other. Again and again. That's what people are like . . . Yet they could be different if they wanted to. But they don't want to. They stone the spirit, they mock it, they abuse life, they crucify it . . . over and over again . . . How senseless it all is! Make themselves poor when they might be rich and not need any divine deliverance . . . the blind fools! Just as if it were bound to be for ever so through the blind turmoil of the ages for centuries and centuries! As if things couldn't be different. As if it had *got* to be. Like ships caught in a maelstrom relentlessly smashing each other to pieces.

Confusion of voices outside. The door is flung open. A crowd of people presses into the room. MAX *at the head.*

MAX: She jumped . . . she jumped . . . she jumped . . . your wife . . . she jumped . . . don't look . . . don't look . . . it's . . . horrible . . .

The body of GRETA HINKEMANN *draped in a sheet is carried into the room.*

HINKEMANN: *with glazed look and mechanical gestures*] Leave me alone, leave me alone . . . Leave me alone with my wife . . . [*Pleading*] Please!

They leave the room. HINKEMANN *goes to the table and takes a ball of string out of the drawer, with great calm he fashions a rope out of the ball of string.*

HINKEMANN: She was healthy and broke through the web. And I still stand here . . . I stand here monstrous and ridiculous . . . In all times there will be men like me. But why me, why pick on me? . . . It strikes at random. This man and that man are stricken. The next and the next again go free . . . What do we know? . . . Where from . . . Where to? . . . Any day can bring the Kingdom of Heaven, any night the End of the World.

CURTAIN